HELP!

I'M OVERWHELMED!

A 4-STEP METHOD
FOR ESCAPING LIFE'S RIP CURRENTS AND
LIVING A PEACEFUL AND MEANINGFUL LIFE

Woody Rini

DOWNLOAD THE H.E.L.P. WORKSHEET AND MENTAL HEALTH RESOURCE WORKSHEET BEFORE YOU START!

I've created a one-page worksheet that you can use to implement my H.E.L.P. method easily. Don't start reading without your H.E.L.P. worksheet in hand!

I've also created a list of every mental health resource I've researched. Never go without mental health resources again!*

For the most up-to-date version of the worksheet and resource list, go to:
http://www.helpimoverwhelmed.com/resources.

No portion of this book, nor any resource provided through the website listed, should be considered professional advice of any kind. Woody Rini and Woody Rini Coaching LLC do not provide therapeutic or medical services. This book and the resources provided through the website listed are not meant to diagnose or treat any disease or disorder of any kind. Third Party resources listed in this book or on the website listed are not endorsed by the author. You are responsible for actions you take.

Trigger warning: this book gives statistics on suicide in chapter two. This book is not meant to treat or prevent suicide. If you are in a severe mental health crisis or are experiencing thoughts of suicide, stop reading this book and call your country's suicide prevention hotline.

To everyone who feels that they are a failure,
or that they are not enough,
or that life is too much to handle:
you have succeeded at far more than you realize,
you are more than enough, and you can handle life—
you just need help.

CONTENTS

CHAPTER ONE

ARE YOU OVERWHELMED?

I hit my overwhelm breaking point in 2016, right before Thanksgiving.

The trigger for this breaking point was a meeting with my boss. I worked as a computer programmer at a large insurance company, and on the last day before the Thanksgiving holiday, I had my performance review. My manager not only gave me a mediocre review but informed me that he didn't really know what projects I was working on. When I left the meeting, we both knew I had no path forward at the company. My career was officially stagnant.

As a response to this poor review, I coped with my overwhelm the way I always did—by playing video games. I'd come home from work and play video games at my apartment all night, snapping at my then-fiancée (now wife), Preetha, if she tried to interrupt. Because my work was going nowhere, winning at video games was my only way to feel like I was actually accomplishing something.

This had been my life since I had entered the workforce a year-and-a-half previously. Deal with overwhelming stress at work, come home, play video games, go to sleep, and repeat.

I also struggled with being overwhelmed in social settings. I had moved from my home state of Kentucky to Preetha's home state of North Carolina a year earlier, so I had few local friends. I attempted to make new friends by joining a nearby church, but I often had panic attacks when church gatherings were held in public places. Once I had to hide in a bathroom at a crowded bar to get away from the noise, the people, and the anxiety that those things caused me. At another social function I had a panic attack and sat on a park bench, far away from everyone else, pretending to check work emails.

The final factor that consistently overwhelmed me was dealing with the challenges of everyday life. I struggled to cook, clean, and maintain a functional apartment. I dealt with health issues such as acid reflux and skin rashes, which caused me constant anxiety and worry. Even small tasks like scheduling appointments and paying bills became overwhelming.

At the time of my overwhelm breaking point in late 2016, my life looked successful and happy to an outside observer. I had a good-paying job, a stable relationship, and maintained at least an appearance of a social life.

But on the inside, I was totally occupied with one thought: "Life is *just too much for me.*"

Going to a job that I struggled with every day was *just too much.*

Dealing with my social anxiety and panic attacks was *just too much.*

Handling my physical issues and illnesses was *just too much.*

And, of course, trying to live a functional adult life full of chores, cooking, cleaning, and bills, all while coping with these stressors, left me feeling like *life itself was just too much.*

If I kept living this way, the overwhelm would slowly crush me until I was a nonfunctional ball of anxiety. My overwhelm would also keep me from ever realizing my true potential, whatever that was.

Worst of all, I had to accept that because my life looked so great on the outside, nobody would ever notice this overwhelm crushing me until it was too late. It was on me to step up and change something about my life.

So, in late 2016, I decided to embark on a multi-year journey to learn everything there was to know about living a happy and successful life. During the first year of my exploration, I read books on happiness and tried meditative and spiritual self-improvement techniques. I attended coaching programs and seminars that promised to help me make money as an entrepreneur.

I learned a lot from this process. I learned about psychology. I learned about business. I learned about managing a household. I became a little happier, and a little more successful. But no matter how much I learned, and no matter how much I tried to use this knowledge to change my life, I still couldn't escape the feeling that life was still too much for me. I felt like I was being dragged out to sea on a powerful current that could pull me under at any moment. At the end of the day, this sense of overwhelm still dogged my every step.

After failing to become significantly happier or more successful in my life by learning on my own, I realized something: I didn't care about being particularly happy or successful, I just wanted *relief from feeling overwhelmed.* I thought, "If I could only feel relaxed and at peace every day, I wouldn't care about my success. I wouldn't care what people thought of me. And I wouldn't even care if I was always on a happy cloud. I just want this overwhelm to go away!"

Having had this realization, my next step was clear: I needed to escape the situation that was overwhelming me most and leave my unfulfilling job. It was time to start interviewing for new positions!

At first, I applied to one or two jobs in my area. I worried and worried about whether I would be the perfect fit. I tried so hard to ace my interviews. I tried to use every interview tactic and personal development technique I had learned through my year of reading and listening to self-improvement seminars. Yet I did not succeed in acquiring a job.

When that didn't work, I finally accepted that I needed to try something new. Namely, I needed to try applying to *many* jobs, however many it took, and that I needed to *ask for help instead of going it alone in my job search.*

I started by asking Preetha to help me edit my cover letter and résumé. She created a beautiful résumé for me and edited the cover letter so that it sounded professional and persuasive. Next, I applied to over twenty jobs in my local area. Some of the jobs weren't even in my field. Some of the jobs were above my pay grade. Some were below. But I was determined to try as many things as I could to see what worked.

Out of the twenty-some jobs I applied to, I received three phone interviews. While I gave my best effort at each interview, I failed to get a job offer. I was frustrated and at my wit's end.

Then, as I was walking my dog at the dog park near my apartment, I got to talking with a friend out with her border collie. I asked her, "Where do you work?"

She replied, "Company X." I suddenly realized that I had sent an application to Company X and hadn't heard back yet. While Company X had over ten thousand employees worldwide, I figured I'd at least ask if she had heard of the hiring manager for my position. Her response shocked me—she not only knew the hiring manager, she worked with him on a regular basis in the same building.

My friend forwarded my résumé to the hiring manager, and the rest was history. Thanks to my failures at previous interviews, I was particularly strong at the interviews for the Company X position. I realized that this job was much better than the other jobs I had wanted. And I got an offer, which I accepted.

I had failed many times, and I had not accomplished anything solely on my own merit. Instead, I asked for help, kept trying, and was lucky enough to cross paths with the right friend at the right time.

It seemed like a messy solution, but asking for help worked far better than trying to be perfect and doing things alone.

Best of all, I felt immense relief when I accepted my new job offer. Being less overwhelmed at work felt so good that I decided to try asking for help in more areas of my life. I decided to ask for help with my mental health issues by signing up for therapy. After talking to my new therapist for a few months, I got a psychiatrist, who gave me additional help in the form of mental health medication.

As life went on, even though I felt panicked and overwhelmed a lot of the time, I kept committing to asking for more help. When I eventually discovered my passion for leading others to live their best lives, I hired a life coach to help me quit my job at Company X and become an entrepreneur. I also asked a successful local businessman to teach me how to run my business. I joined peer support groups that helped me deal with my mental health issues.

Asking for help has done what every self-improvement technique in the world could not do for me: it has given me lasting relief from being overwhelmed and made me feel that life is not too much—that I am enough, and that I can handle everyday life.

I still have challenges daily. I still struggle with career, social, and sensory issues. But each day, by asking for more help from others, I become a little less overwhelmed. I can work calmly and steadily toward my career goals. I can breathe deeply and be at peace at social functions that before would leave me huddled in a bathroom crying. I am even able to do more chores, cook and clean, and handle personal finances, bills, and appointments without panicking. As a result of this, I'm a more loving husband, a better friend, and a more helpful member of society.

There is a solution to being overwhelmed, and the solution is to ask for help. The relief that comes from implementing this solution is, in my opinion, the best feeling in life.

AM I OVERWHELMED?

In order to help you decide if this book is for you, I'd like to clearly define what being overwhelmed means in the context of this book.

You are overwhelmed if you feel you're being asked to take on more than you can handle.

In my career, I felt overwhelmed because I was being asked to work hard at a job where my individual talents weren't seen or used properly, and I couldn't handle watching my talents go to waste.

In my social life, I felt overwhelmed because I was being asked to make small talk at large gatherings full of noise and chaos, and I couldn't handle the stimulation of the social environment.

In my home life, I felt overwhelmed because I was being asked to do chores, pay bills, cook, clean, and take care of my dog, all while maintaining my job (which overwhelmed me) and my social life (which overwhelmed me), and I didn't feel like I could handle all of that at once.

I started to live in a state of perpetual overwhelm that was marked by specific symptoms:

- a general thought that "life is too much!"
- resentment against the world for asking too much of me, accompanied by occasional emotional meltdowns
- chronic anxiety due to constantly evaluating when I would run out of energy and whether I could perform a given task without breaking down

- panic and frenetic action to try to escape stress, followed by numbing my feelings through alcohol or screen time

As I refer throughout this book to your "overwhelm," I mean your tendencies to think, feel, and act as described above, brought about by a long-running sense of being overwhelmed. It's a little weird to see "overwhelm" used as a noun, but think of it like the word "burnout." When someone is exhausting themselves—when they're burning out their mental fuel—for long enough, they experience burnout. Similarly, when someone is overwhelmed for long enough, they experience overwhelm.

LASTING RELIEF FROM OVERWHELM IS POSSIBLE: YOU JUST NEED H.E.L.P.

So, if you're overwhelmed and you need help in order to find relief, how do you get it? Simple: you use the H.E.L.P. method!

The H.E.L.P. method is what I use in life to replicate the success I had in escaping from my work overwhelm. It's based on the idea that life is so overwhelming that we must ask for help from others. Asking for help is scary, but H.E.L.P. makes it easy by breaking it down into four basic steps.

When you take the steps that H.E.L.P. offers, you'll find that you slowly build a structure of people who support you and keep you safe. As your helpers take stress off your plate, the state of overwhelm you've lived in will slowly shift toward a state of peace. Once you find relief from your overwhelm, you'll also be free to spend more time pursuing your passions and developing a life that feels meaningful to you.

Here's how the structure of this book prepares you to implement the H.E.L.P. method.

In chapter two, you'll get exposed to the analogy that frames H.E.L.P., the analogy of the rip current. This analogy will give you clear and simple language that helps you react to your overwhelm productively. You'll also learn about the one-page H.E.L.P. worksheet you can use to work through the four steps.

In chapter three, you'll learn how modern society's individualistic school and work systems set us up to believe the "Ultimate Overwhelming Thought" (that we are failures if we don't get things right on the first try) and how to change your mindset to the "Ultimate Empowering Thought" (that we can try as many times as we want, with as much help as we can get, to find a way to meet our needs).

In chapter four, you'll learn the first H.E.L.P. technique: Halt the Panic. You'll learn why acting out of panic only makes things worse, and how to stop yourself from panicking in the face of your overwhelming challenges.

In chapter five, you'll learn the second H.E.L.P. technique: Engage Emotions. You'll learn why most of us choose to "drown" our emotions using drugs, screen time, or other numbing behaviors instead of engaging our emotions to solve problems. You'll then learn why emotions are a valuable tool, and you'll commit to engaging them.

In chapter six, you'll learn the third H.E.L.P. technique: Look for Help. This chapter teaches you exactly how to find the help you need to reduce your overwhelm, showing you the ways to make use of umbrella people, peer support groups, therapists, and more.

In chapter seven, you'll learn the fourth H.E.L.P. technique: Patiently Float and Parallel Swim. You'll learn how patiently floating along can often bring you out of your overwhelming situations, and how to be productive without fighting battles you can't win.

Finally, in chapter eight, you'll learn about Enjoying the Beach. You'll learn how finding relief from overwhelm will bring you peace and reduce the negative consequences you experienced from being overwhelmed. You'll also learn how a life with less overwhelm is a life where you can find deeper personal meaning, and how getting help makes you a giver, not a taker.

Ultimately, if you're overwhelmed and you want to feel relief, then this is the book for you. Let's get started!

CHAPTER TWO

YOU NEED H.E.L.P.

I magine for a moment you're at an ocean beach. You see the waves come from a distance, break against the shore, and fade back into the ocean. This is how the water normally flows. If you get into the water at the beach and swim around, you'll generally either float in place or be washed back toward land by the waves.

There's one area of the ocean where water behaves differently, however. Rip currents, also sometimes mistakenly called rip tides or undertows, occur in large bodies of water such as oceans and the Great Lakes. These narrow channels quickly draw water back toward the ocean. When a swimmer enters a part of the water where a rip current exists, they're pulled away from the beach. Imagine paddling around, enjoying the water, and suddenly finding yourself farther away from the beach than you realized! This is what happens when a person swims in a rip current.

If you were in the ocean and found yourself being pulled away from the beach by a current of water, what would you do? Simple—you'd swim toward the beach with all your might! Your instincts would be screaming, "Swim as fast as you can back to shore! If you get dragged into the ocean, you'll drown and die!"

There's only one problem with this seemingly straightforward strategy: if the current is flowing faster than you can swim, you'll never make it back to shore. Instead, you'll spend all your strength frantically fighting the unbeatable current, eventually succumbing to exhaustion. Even though your instincts have good intentions (getting you back to shore), they instead cause you to panic and drown. Sadly, over a hundred swimmers per year drown in rip currents in the US alone. That's more than die from shark attacks!

The good news is that far more swimmers are rescued from rip currents than drown from them. Tens of thousands of swimmers escape from rip currents every year. How do these swimmers escape a current that flows faster than they can swim? They ask for help and are rescued by a lifeguard.

There's a protocol taught to all swimmers in the ocean for how to react to a rip current: "Wave, Yell, Swim Parallel." This is the swimmer's version of H.E.L.P., and what I've based my method on. First, the swimmer stops panicking against the current. Second, the swimmer yells for help as loud as they can while waving their arms. Finally, the swimmer floats along with the current or swims parallel to the beach, out of the current, until they can be rescued. This protocol is counterintuitive. After all, swimming directly at the shore, the goal, actually gets the swimmer killed! And asking for help while letting themselves float farther from the shore saves the swimmer's life.

Life's Overwhelm Currents Are Just as Deadly as Rip Currents

The H.E.L.P. method outlined in this book is based on the logic that life's overwhelming challenges operate just like rip currents and are just as deadly. Therefore, we should not fight against life directly when it's overwhelming us. Instead, we should call for help and float patiently, maybe swimming sideways a little to get out of the worst of it while help comes to rescue us from our overwhelm current.

Rip currents kill more than one hundred US swimmers annually, but this number pales in comparison to the number of people who lose their lives each year to overwhelm currents. According to the CDC, around forty-six thousand people lost their lives to suicide in 2020 in the United States alone. Here are some more statistics on suicide in the US from 2020:

> Suicide is a leading cause of death in the United States, with 45,979 deaths in 2020. This is about one death every 11 minutes. The number of people who think about or attempt suicide is even higher. In 2020, an estimated 12.2 million American adults seriously thought about suicide, 3.2 million planned a suicide attempt, and 1.2 million attempted suicide.
> (https://www.cdc.gov/suicide/facts/)

*** Remember, if you are considering or planning a suicide attempt, this book is not the right resource for you. Please set this book down and visit the US National Suicide Prevention Hotline (https://suicidepreventionlifeline.org/) or the appropriate website or hotline for your country of residence
(https://en.wikipedia.org/wiki/List_of_suicide_crisis_lines)

immediately. This book is not meant to treat any mental disorder or prevent suicide. ***

As sobering as the number of people who consider suicide is, it's a mere fraction of the people in the US who suffer from mental health disorders. According to the CDC's 2018 data, there were 55.7 *million* visits to primary care physicians in 2018 where the primary diagnosis was a mental health disorder. (https://www.cdc.gov/nchs/fastats/mental-health.htm) In fact, I was one of these people. It was 2018 when my primary care physician referred me to therapy.

I believe that our society has an epidemic of mental health issues, even suicide, *because we all feel overwhelmed.*

Here's how I think it happens: life situations place stress on us by asking us to do so many exhausting things, which overwhelm us when that stress is too much to handle. We then experience negative consequences such as anxiety, depression, panic, and physical pain.

Thus the pattern we must escape is: experience stress → stress reaches a breaking point and we become overwhelmed → we start to live in a state of constant overwhelm → we feel anxious, depressed, ill, and even suicidal.

Even if you don't become clinically anxious or depressed, you're still probably experiencing serious symptoms of being overwhelmed. Some of the everyday consequences are:

- getting stuck in a job you don't like because just applying for a new one would burn you out
- losing sleep thinking about life's constant demands, causing a cycle of daily fatigue that affects the rest of your life

- experiencing conflict in your relationships because your overwhelm is spilling onto the people you care about
- feeling afraid to go out in public, where the stimulation of social situations is more than you can handle
- being unable to attend to your physical health because you're too swamped to take time for self-care
- never discovering your true potential because you have no energy to explore your gifts and talents

As you can see, you don't have to be suicidal or clinically diagnosed with anxiety or depression to experience a wide range of overwhelm symptoms.

Because the spectrum of negative health consequences from overwhelm is so large, finding relief is the best personal improvement goal to shoot for. This is a better goal than happiness or success because when you find relief from overwhelm, you'll not only relieve many negative consequences, you'll naturally become happier and more successful! Reducing overwhelm is the key piece of the puzzle that makes for a peaceful and meaningful life.

THREE PRINCIPLES OF HOW ASKING FOR HELP REALLY WORKS

While life's challenges may be as scary as a rip current, take heart in the fact that good help can save us where we can't save ourselves. Let's look quickly at the characteristics of asking for help as it applies to rip currents so that we can adapt it for handling life's overwhelm currents.

First of all, the swimmers trapped in rip currents wave and yell for help with *desperation and passion*. If I'm trapped in a rip current and I need someone to save my life, I'm not going to mess around. I'm not going to do a little polite wave and a quiet request. I'm going to shout at the top of my lungs, "HELP!!! I'M DROWNING!!!" I do so because I know it's a life-or-death mission.

Second, notice how the swimmer *just needs one person's attention in order to get saved.* If only one beachgoer notices the cry for help, that beachgoer can inform the lifeguard, who can come out and save the swimmer. When I first asked for help with my job interview process, I found an unexpected resource (my friend at the apartment) because I was willing to keep speaking up about my overwhelming problem.

Third, notice that the person asking for help is asking for real, tangible support. They are not asking for information or advice. Imagine if a swimmer was trapped in a rip current and a lifeguard simply stood on the beach and said, "You're not swimming hard enough! Why can't you be as good as I am? Go that way!" It wouldn't make any sense. The drowning, panicking swimmer doesn't need information. They need someone to jump into the water and bring them back to shore, which is exactly what lifeguards do.

As we go through the H.E.L.P. method, we're going to apply these principles to dealing with everyday life. You're going to learn to shout, "Help! I'm overwhelmed!" whenever you feel yourself in a current. You're going to learn to keep asking for help, because if you can get *even one person's attention, you can be saved.* And you're going to learn that when you ask for help, you're asking for *tangible safety and support, not for advice or information.* These principles form the core of H.E.L.P.

WHY DEDICATED, TRAINED HELPERS ARE SO CRITICAL TO GETTING HELP

We must recognize that just like swimmers need dedicated lifeguards to save them, people in overwhelm currents need dedicated helpers to rescue them as well. When a person is drowning, they will cling to anything and anyone they can. Unfortunately, a panicking, drowning swimmer may actually end up drowning both themselves and their helper if the helper is not prepared. (https://www.usla.org/page/RIPCUR-RENTS) That's why the best thing to do at the beach when someone is trapped in a rip current is to call for a lifeguard instead of trying to help them yourself.

But what is it about lifeguards that makes them so specially equipped to rescue people? They have three advantages that everyday beachgoers don't have: perspective, training, and specialized tools.

Lifeguards sit in a tall chair so that they can have a wide and accurate perspective of what's going on in the water. Not only can the lifeguard better see where the individual swimmers are, they can also see where rip currents might form. Rips are much easier to spot from an aerial view. This means that when a lifeguard rescues someone from a rip current, they know how to get that person out of the current safely.

Lifeguards also have specialized training. They are tested thoroughly to ensure they're strong swimmers. Where a regular beachgoer might not be able to navigate the turbulent ocean, a lifeguard can swim quickly and efficiently to the drowning swimmer and rescue them.

Finally, lifeguards have specialized tools. In particular, they have flotation devices. Lifeguards don't go into the water empty-handed. When they reach the drowning swimmer, they don't ask the swimmer to grab onto them, which risks drowning them both. Instead, they give the swimmer a large flotation device to hold onto, and then they paddle back to shore with the swimmer safely in tow.

As you can see, the difference between an unprepared fellow swimmer and a lifeguard trying to rescue a drowning swimmer can be stark. The fellow swimmer may simply drown along with their companion, while the lifeguard can rescue the drowning swimmer using their combination of perspective, training, and specialized tools.

I believe that professional help is equally as important when we're navigating life's overwhelm currents. We need to seek dedicated professionals to provide the help we need. These may include therapists, doctors, personal trainers, physical therapists, massage therapists, chiropractors, nutritionists, life and business coaches, and any number of other trained professionals who possess vital resources just as lifeguards do.

Dedicated professionals have perspective. For example, a therapist may have the vantage point needed to spot a mental disorder you didn't know you have. After all, while your experiences might seem normal and healthy through your eyes, your therapist can recognize unhealthy coping mechanisms, symptoms of mental illness, and past trauma. I didn't know I had generalized anxiety disorder until I met with a therapist who had the skills to spot that disorder in me!

Professionals also are trained with substantial education and practice, allowing them to implement specific techniques of care. I recently had severe back pain and tried to resolve it myself by stretching and sitting differently. But no matter what I did, I wasn't able to heal my aching body. I was so disheartened and overwhelmed by this pain! But after two visits to a massage therapist and my chiropractor, my back pain disappeared. Why? Because the professionals had the know-how and skills to understand, adjust, and ultimately change my body in ways I never could have accomplished myself.

Finally, professionals are always prepared with the tools needed for the job. Therapists have extensive, proven systems for modifying behavior and reducing mental health problems. Nutritionists have healthy eating worksheets and supplements to keep health challenges at bay. Psychiatrists have diagnostic instruments and medications to alleviate chemical imbalances in the brain. Doctors and dentists, of course, have their own array of machines and gadgets! All professionals come with tools that make the difference between life and death.

If professionals are so critical to giving people help, it begs the question: how do we, as non-professionals, help those in our network who need support? What should we do when we encounter a friend, family member, or student battling an overwhelming challenge that we aren't qualified to deal with on our own? What do we do when finding professional help for someone we love would take time and money that we don't have, and we're all that someone has for now?

The answer is the same as that for someone rescuing a drowning swimmer. We need to avoid trying to take on their burden as our own, instead offering the best floatation device we can find. The crucial rule in water rescue is at all costs avoid direct skin-to skin-contact. Offer anything that floats to a drowning person and they will instinctively grab on, so it's best to offer a flotation device, which can save them, rather than your hand, which could end up drowning you both.

We need to do the same thing with others who are over-whelmed. Rather than jumping in and trying to be a savior, we need to give them the best floatation devices we can find. It may be a book, a support group, or tangible help.

But whatever we do to help, we must set a crystal-clear boundary that separates ourselves from the other person. We may help them with their overwhelm, but we must not claim it as our own. Otherwise, instead of helping them, we'll just be drowning along with them. Resources for finding profes-sional help within time and money constraints, as well as more ways you can help the people in your life who need it, will be provided in chapter six.

INTRODUCING THE H.E.L.P. METHOD

Now that we've created a frame of reference around the rip current analogy, we can finally consider what it looks like to get H.E.L.P. in facing the overwhelm currents that everyday life throws at us.

The H.E.L.P. method is an acronym for a four-step pro-cess that's analogous to the steps swimmers take to be rescued from rip currents.

H stands for "Halt the Panic"
E stands for "Engage Emotions"
L stands for "Look for Help"
P stands for "Patiently Float" or "Parallel Swim"
When used correctly, these tools are lifesavers.

H IS FOR "HALT THE PANIC"

The first thing we need to do when we realize we're over-whelmed is stop panicking. Just like a swimmer needs to stop fighting the current head on, we need to stop directly fighting our issues when they're stronger than we are. If we fight a battle we can't win, we only make things worse. We need to identify the specific panic behaviors we do and how to stop them.

E IS FOR "ENGAGE EMOTIONS"

In rip currents, swimmers who cannot keep swimming drown. While a small minority of people trapped in overwhelm currents do sadly choose to end their own lives, the vast majority of people remain physically alive, but drown in a more subtle way. I call this "drowning emotions," and it occurs when we try to numb our emotions by distracting ourselves from them through seeking excessive stimulation. Instead, we must engage our emotions and recognize them for the powerful, positive tools that they are.

L IS FOR "LOOK FOR HELP"

I wish that "help" was spelled "heYp," because I wanted to make this section "YELL for help!" As we covered earlier, we must yell for help at the top of our lungs. But we must also be willing to look for help wherever it might come from. Like the trapped swimmer who only needs one person to see their call in order to notify the lifeguard, we only need one person to hear our cry in order to begin getting help.

There's a reason I named this book *Help! I'm Overwhelmed!* I believe that those three words contain the solution to life's problems. If we just keep saying those words, we'll find a way to meet our needs. In this chapter we'll see exactly how to do so by engaging friends, support groups, and professionals.

P IS FOR "PATIENTLY FLOAT" AND "PARALLEL SWIM"

While yelling for help is our main source of relief from overwhelm, we'll need to do something while we wait for the help to come. In the deep dive on this section, I'll offer a variety of techniques for how you can stay buoyant instead of fighting against your overwhelm currents.

Some of these techniques will be "float techniques," which means they'll be aimed solely at keeping you patiently afloat while you're in the middle of crisis. Other techniques will be "parallel swim" techniques, which means they'll help you make progress out of your current, but not by fighting directly against it. At the end of the chapter, you'll know what to do while you wait for help to come.

H.E.L.P. CAN BRING YOU RELIEF

What happens when you use the H.E.L.P. techniques to escape your overwhelm currents? You get to feel the most amazing feeling in the world: relief. Imagine a swimmer rescued from drowning by a lifeguard. The moment they land on the shore, they aren't worrying about trivial details. They aren't stressed about yesterday or tomorrow. They're feeling one thing: immense gladness that they're still alive. Just being on solid ground is enough for them.

I believe that if you use the H.E.L.P. techniques, you'll feel the same as that swimmer when you're helped out of your own overwhelm currents. You won't be worried about trivial matters like what people think about you or whether you're "a success" or not. You won't be stressed about proving yourself to others. You won't feel like a failure. You'll feel the pure, blissful relief of being on solid ground.

I've started to feel this bliss, this relief, more and more as I've used these techniques for myself. This feeling has outstripped all other things: success, achievement, pleasure. I don't want those things anymore. I just want relief from overwhelm and the peace that comes with it. You can find this feeling too.

Using Your H.E.L.P. Worksheet

This book is meant be used alongside the one-page H.E.L.P. worksheet I've created for you (found in the appendix of this book or at http://www.helpimoverwhelmed.com/resources for a printable copy). As you read *Help! I'm Overwhelmed!*, simply fill out the corresponding portion of this H.E.L.P. worksheet when prompted.

At the end of the book, you'll have completed your very first H.E.L.P. cycle. By answering the prompts and making the commitments to get help, you'll move from panicked, drowning, and overwhelmed to supported, safe, and peaceful. The only requirements for successfully completing H.E.L.P. are being honest in your answers and being willing to get help. That's it!

You can use a new H.E.L.P. worksheet whenever you face another overwhelming challenge. I've created a lot of these documents over the years in my attempt to improve my quality of life, and I can confidently say that the H.E.L.P. worksheet is my best yet. In the months preceding this book launch, I used it to help me tackle issues like book-writing overwhelm, body image fears, and relationship issues. In this book's appendix, you'll find a sample of a filled-out worksheet, which shows the steps I took to get out of career overwhelm. I know that the H.E.L.P. worksheet works because I use it myself!

However, the H.E.L.P. method is not a quick-fix solution and does not guarantee any specific results. There is no secret or special technique that will make your problems go away overnight. H.E.L.P. takes patience because you'll need time to engage the various helpers in your life. You'll also notice that the H.E.L.P. method asks you to make commitments. For example, when you read the worksheet's section on finding a peer support group, you'll see that there's a blank for you to write down what peer support group you'll attend, at what time, and at what place. There's no way to fake a H.E.L.P. worksheet short of lying! Rather than asking you to reflect in a general way, H.E.L.P. asks you to commit to taking specific, actionable steps toward a better life.

So, print off your H.E.L.P. worksheet or pull it up online, and let's get to work!

CHAPTER THREE

HOW MODERN SCHOOL SYSTEMS AND WORKPLACES SET US UP TO BE OVERWHELMED

I n this chapter we'll cover how society's systems create a foundation for later overwhelm. Specifically, we'll explore how school and work use individual performance measurements and "one try at perfection" grading to evaluate us, and how these two things make us overwhelmed.

After exploring these topics, we'll look at how the overwhelm created by school and work causes us to have the Ultimate Overwhelming Thought: "I should be able to do this perfectly the first time, by myself, but I can't, *so I am a failure.*"

We'll then take a look at how our personal lives don't operate under individualism or "one try at perfection" thinking, and how they instead operate as the opposite: as part of a larger system that can help us, and with as many tries as we can take in order to meet our needs.

We'll see how instead we can think the Ultimate Empowering Thought: "I can try this thing as many times as I want, with as much help as I can find, *until I find a way to meet my need.*"

I hope you'll leave this chapter with the understanding that while you're part of a society whose institutions overwhelm you, asking for help can relieve you of this overwhelm and allow you to achieve things you never thought possible.

HOW SCHOOL ASSIGNMENTS AND MEASUREMENTS OVERWHELM STUDENTS

My friend's daughter, Alice, is six years old and a very smart girl. She asks insightful questions, such as, "Where do we go when we die?" She knows an enormous amount about the animal kingdom, constantly wishing to have a "prehensile tail" (the kind monkeys use to hang from branches). She's athletic, imaginative, courageous, and smart. But she's already becoming overwhelmed by school.

In her kindergarten class, Alice is asked to read one book per week. And she struggles with some of these reading assignments. My friend tells me that sometimes Alice has a temper tantrum in the middle of reading and decides she doesn't want to do it anymore because it's too much for her. In other words, Alice, at a mere six years old, feels overwhelmed by the modern school system.

The overwhelm Alice feels when trying to complete a reading assignment is no fault of her parents or teacher. Both are exceedingly patient. My friend is excellent with Alice, finding new, creative ways for her to practice reading without feeling pressure. Alice's teacher is kind and gentle (as most teachers are!), identifying Alice's gifts and drawing those out. No individual is trying to overwhelm Alice or hold her to a standard that she can't live up to.

The responsibility for Alice's overwhelm lies not at the hands of any malicious individual—it's simply a side effect of the modern school system. Assignments are given, students have a set time to complete them, and then they're graded on a scale where the goal is perfection (usually 100/100). While my friend's kindergartener might not be graded particularly harshly, students at most higher levels of school are.

Schools value academic performance on specific cognitive-based assignments, completed as individuals without help, with one chance to get a grade that's measured toward perfection and then competitively evaluated against their peers. This is quite the overwhelming task!

Students who struggle at reading or standardized test formats are consistently overwhelmed because they're asked to excel at something within a rigid, punitive structure. But equally as dangerously, top students too are overwhelmed as they're constantly asked to take the "next step" in an increasingly competitive education system.

Top high school students, who are considered models of success, duke it out to get into top colleges. College students compete academically for the best graduate school résumé, with those having the highest GPA being considered the most successful. Grad students compete for research assistantships, fellowships, and other exclusive scholarships, as well as placement in PhD programs. PhD students work earnestly on their dissertations hoping to land a prestigious teaching job. Heck, even professors must compete and prove their worth in order to receive tenure.

Because of the competitive nature of each stage of school, there's rarely a standard of "good enough." Instead, the standard is perfection, or sometimes higher than perfection. At high schools, a 4.0 generally indicates that a student has received all A's—a perfect GPA. But at my wife's high school, students who took AP and Honors classes could receive weighted grades that gave them a GPA above 4.0. Successful students would battle to take and earn an A in as many AP classes as they could to receive 6.0 and 5.0 grades, hoping to secure the spot of valedictorian and ensure they got into prestigious colleges. Preetha graduated high school with all A's and a 5.4 weighted GPA yet only ranked fifth in her high school graduating class.

Imagine the pressure of knowing that no matter how hard you work, even if you achieve a standard *above* perceived perfection, someone else may still rank higher than you. Then realize that if you grew up in the modern school system, you probably experienced that pressure!

If that isn't enough to worry you about how schools hold students to impossible standards, consider this: some undergraduate and graduate courses grade on a curve, meaning that only a certain number of students can receive an A in a class. Preetha's law school did this, and when Preetha was in advanced classes with the rest of the top achievers, she received a lower grade not because her own work was insufficient but because she was not quite as good as the other excellent students.

Because there is no reasonable standard of "good enough" in the academic world, and because students

only get one chance at most tests or assignments, students must constantly give everything they have to optimize their chance at receiving a top grade.

This never-ending ask for more is a sure recipe for disaster, because no matter how much students can handle, more will always be thrown at them until they're finally overwhelmed.

How School Measurements Lead to Overwhelm Breaking Points

A personal story about my overwhelm breakdown, resulting in a major depressive episode, illustrates the consequences of academic overwhelm well.

I attended Centre College, a liberal arts school in Danville, Kentucky, and as a freshman I was one of the top students in my grade. I had been one of three students in my entire class to receive a 4.0, a perfect grade, for my entire first year. I was immensely proud of this. After all, I knew that I'd never get a chance to redo my GPA, and I knew that I'd be competing against other students for jobs in the future, so I figured that having a 4.0 gave me the best chance of getting a good job and thus having a happy life. I perceived my GPA as quite literally a measurement of future success.

But sometime in the spring of my sophomore year, I became overwhelmed. My work was piling up, and no matter how hard I tried to read every page of assigned reading and complete every assignment perfectly, I just couldn't do it. There simply wasn't enough time in the day to get everything done while also living up to my duties as a Resident Assistant, a member of the tennis team, and a member of my fraternity. I was asking myself to do more than I could handle.

You guessed it—I was Overwhelmed, with a capital O. But because nobody else could do my schoolwork for me, I never considered asking for help in any way. And because I knew that I was being measured against perfection, a 4.0, I never considered trying to shoot for a lower goal. So I started waking up earlier and staying up later trying to do everything. I vividly remember being awake at 6:30 a.m., drinking coffee in the campus center, trying to read the last few pages of my religion reading to prepare for a test at 8 a.m. But as I walked into the classroom and started taking the exam, my body decided that it had reached a breaking point. I was hit with a wave of major depression. My mind was in a complete fog. I answered a few of the questions, and then came to the essay question worth fifty percent of the grade. But my body couldn't do it anymore. So I wrote, "I can't do this" on my essay and handed the test in. I then went outside, sat on a mound of grass, and cried. It was pouring rain. All of the overwhelm had finally caught up to me, and I was starting to experience the mental health symptoms that come from chronic overwhelm.

What happened next wasn't pretty: I went into a major depressive episode. I became unable to go to class or get out of bed. My mom had to come visit the school to help me. I was referred to the school therapist and put on medication for depression. I had to visit the dean of the college to ask if I could redo certain assignments. After a few weeks of taking it easy and a week of spring break, I recovered. Because I was very lucky, I was able to retake my religion test, a chance rarely offered to students.

But even though I healed from my depression, I never really understood that what had happened to me wasn't my fault. In my head, I'd ruined my chance at a 4.0, which ruined my chance at being valedictorian, which ruined my chance to achieve my full potential.

I thought that I needed to be perfect on the first try, without any help, in order to be successful. I had failed at that, and thus I was a failure.

I didn't understand that I needed help, or perhaps H.E.L.P., in order to survive a school system whose very nature overwhelms nearly all its students.

HOW MODERN WORKPLACE RANKING SYSTEMS CAUSE OVERWHELM

As you may remember from my story in the introductory chapter, the modern workplace caused me just as much overwhelm as the school system. Because I knew I was going to be given an annual evaluation at the end of the year, I was constantly anxious about how well I was doing my job. If I was slammed with work, I was stressed that I'd be judged for asking for help. If I didn't have enough work, I was stressed that I wouldn't accomplish enough work in the year, and thus receive a worse evaluation.

To top this off, my work evaluation was graded on a curve just like my wife's law school. When people are graded on a curve in the workplace it's called "stack ranking," and it has a variety of overwhelming side effects. Stack ranking gives employees constant anxiety about performance, causes them to feel resentful when their work goes unseen, and encourages both employees and managers to "manage up" by pretending they're doing more work than they actually are.

Worse, sometimes stack ranking systems cause outright sabotage between members of the same company. Employees might withhold vital information from a coworker because they know that they're being ranked against them at the end of the year. Paradoxically, the company's attempt to rank the employees to improve performance ends up hurting the performance of all employees. When Preetha was touring law schools as a prospective student, one law school (which also used stack ranking for grades) boasted that "this is not a law school where students rip pages out of each other's textbooks." The implication was that at many top law schools, this was a common practice.

HOW PRESSURE FOR CONSTANT AVAILABILITY AT WORK CAUSES OVERWHELM

The other factor contributing to employee overwhelm is the constant pressure to be available. Whether a person works at a private company, for a government, or for a different entity, they're often asked to be available regardless of the time of day.

With the rise of the internet, smartphones, and working from home has come a blurring of lines between work and home life. In my definition of overwhelm in the first chapter, I mentioned that people experiencing overwhelm must constantly evaluate whether they have the energy to perform another task. This is now true of work even when you're home! If you're at home, enjoying an evening episode of television, and your boss calls and asks you to work more, do you say yes or no? In previous times, the answer likely would have been no, partially because you wouldn't have had the ability to work from home, and partially because going into the office would have been too much to ask at night.

But with modern-day work-from-home culture, there's more pressure to be available at different times of the day. After all, you probably have at least one internet-connected device nearby at all times. Couldn't you spend five minutes to pop out that one work email? The overwhelm that comes from working from home isn't merely from working more; it's also from having to constantly decide whether to work more or not, and what it means for your career. You may feel like saying yes to work at 8 p.m. could be the thing that gets you promoted and secures your future.

It's not just private firm members who struggle with the burden of an increasingly complex online work system: teachers, for example, are also suffering ill-effects from working from home. According to psychology journal *Frontiers in Psychology*, middle school teachers experienced significantly more burnout during COVID-19-induced work from home periods than before the pandemic. (Gutentag and Asterhan, 2022) While teachers likely won't have to work totally from home or deal with COVID-19 forever, they'll probably have to become more proficient at an increasing number of online technologies while making themselves available to parents and administrators at all hours. Pandemic or not, the same work-from-home, 24/7-access-to-technology lifestyle will remain in our culture across many types of jobs.

Modern workers face the same dilemma that modern students do: they are being evaluated by their performance compared to others, and they're being asked to perform more and more labor. No matter how much they work on a given day, they must always decide whether they want to work more that day or not. This continuous decision-making is exhausting, and ultimately it's too much for anyone to handle alone, so it causes overwhelm.

SCHOOL AND WORK TEACH US TO BELIEVE WE ARE FAILURES

I believe that because of the way school and work operate in modern society, we are all falsely taught to believe that we are failures.

We believe that we must achieve a standard of perfection, or else we are a failure.

We believe that we must excel at tests and performance reviews, based on only our own merits, and always achieve a top grade, or else we are failures.

And we are always asked for more by both schools and the workplace. We are asked to study more, to achieve more, to work more or longer hours in worse conditions. If we can't handle that, we are failures.

When we cannot meet these standards and we eventually break, we then think the Ultimate Overwhelming Thought: "I should be able to do this perfectly the first time, but I can't, so *I am a failure.*"

Or, in another variation, we might think, "I should be able to work harder and longer, but I can't, *so I am a failure.*"

When we say these thoughts to ourselves and agree with them, what we are really saying is this: "I should be able to do the impossible, but I can't, *so I am a failure.*"

What I wish I had been taught at a young age was that the demands of school and work were always going to be impossible. But I didn't know it then, and many of us don't know it now.

I hope that by seeing this evidence, you now see that you have been asked to do the impossible your whole life and considered it normal. You have believed that the Ultimate Overwhelming Thought is true and run yourself ragged trying to get things right on the first try. This is why you're overwhelmed.

I don't say this to blame the school or work systems. This book is not about how we can overhaul these institutions. School relies on a grading system to measure how students are doing. Workplaces rely on employee measurements to make sure employees are doing their job. Our modern, specialized world demands these ranking systems, even as smart people are already working to dismantle school grading and workplace ranking.

But the amazing news I'm about to share with you is this: regardless of what schools and companies do, we don't need to live our individual lives in this impossible and overwhelmed manner. In our personal lives, we can ask for help and try things as many times as we want. And as we practice the H.E.L.P. method in our personal lives, we can learn to ask for help within the work and school systems too. Work and school will never perfectly adapt to make us less overwhelmed, so it will be harder to use H.E.L.P. there than in our personal lives, yet we'll slowly but surely learn to maximize our ability to get help in all areas if we keep working at it.

Embracing the Ultimate Empowering Thought

As I mentioned before, the Ultimate Empowering Thought is "I can try this thing as many times as I want, with as much help as I can find, *until I find a way to meet my need.*"

The first way this thought is different than the Ultimate Overwhelming Thought is that instead of saying we "should be able to" do something, we say we "can try" to do something. Saying we "can try" grounds us in the reality that we don't know whether we should be able to do something, while also empowering us by saying we have the capacity to make an attempt.

The second way this thought is different from the Ultimate Overwhelming Thought is that it says we can try "as many times as we want." For example, say you want to play a specific song on the guitar. As long as you can keep your fingers moving, you can keep endeavoring to play the song. There is no limit on how many times you can try! You could do it a thousand times before you learn how to play the song correctly. It's self-evidently true that you can try as much as you want; your guitar doesn't get snatched away after just a few attempts (but your test at school does!).

The truth is that we get as many tries as we can generate. We may be limited by money, sleep, energy, time, or some other resource, but we can try as much as we want until those resources run out. If we're looking to earn more, we can keep trying new business ideas until one works out. If we're overwhelmed by raising our child, we can try new parenting techniques until one works out. When we lose the "one try at perfection" mindset and let ourselves practice something over and over again, we may experiment much more quickly and try many more things than we thought possible. That's definitely been my experience!

The third way the Ultimate Empowering Thought is different from the Ultimate Overwhelming Thought is that instead of saying we must do things "by ourselves," we say that we can use "as much help as we can find." If we need someone's expertise to help us learn the guitar song we're studying, we can hire them as a teacher. If we need more exposure to music, we can go to a concert. If we need someone to pay for the guitar lessons and the concert, we can appeal to our parents or to a friend, or we can ask for help earning more money.

Thinking in terms of asking for help opens up a number of possibilities that were previously closed off. If we were taught the Ultimate Overwhelming Thought in school and tried to learn guitar that way, we might give up after fifteen minutes of solitary practice on the song, thinking ourselves a failure because we didn't get it right on the first try. But if we believe we can ask for as much help as we can find, then we will become energized, searching up lessons, selecting concerts, finding ways to raise money, and forming relationships in the process!

There's one more sneaky but crucial difference between the Ultimate Overwhelming Thought and the Ultimate Empowering Thought: the Ultimate Overwhelming Thought focuses on "doing something right" while the Ultimate Empowering Thought focuses on "meeting a need."

In school and work, we perform tasks in an attempt to do our job "right." We try to answer test questions right or perform work tasks in the right manner. But what is the value in "doing something right"? The thinking goes that if we do enough things right, we'll get a good job and have a stable relationship, at which point we'll be financially secure and happy. What are financial security and happiness? They are *needs*. The Ultimate Overwhelming Thought is so overwhelming because it causes us to lose sight of the fact that "correctness" or "rightness" are only arbitrary guideposts toward the truly important goal of meeting our needs.

Why is this harmful? Because if we're distracted by trying to do things right, we'll fail to see simple ways to meet our needs, getting stuck in complex and overwhelming situations that we never wanted in the first place! Let's pretend for a moment that our person learning the guitar is doing so to impress a potential romantic partner. If they get tunnel vision on playing the guitar right as the only way to meet their need, then they may practice for an hour and give up when they can't do it. The frustration of failing to learn the song hurts because they've unintentionally valued one-try-at-perfection over their actual need of connecting with the potential partner. And when they fail to get the song right, they may feel like a failure overall and never ask that person on a date!

If our guitar player instead focuses on their need (finding a romantic partner), then their journey is much more fun and flexible. They may try to learn the guitar for a while. They may schedule lessons and concerts. But after looking at how much effort it would take to impress their potential partner with guitar skills, or after failing to learn guitar with help, our guitar player may simply find another way to impress their love interest! Perhaps they're a natural at writing poems. Or perhaps they're just a kind person who's easy to talk to. Maybe they finally decide to ask the person out without having any plan at all! It doesn't matter how they find their partner—if they find one solution that works, then their problem is solved.

This is why the Ultimate Empowering Thought is so empowering: it teaches us that even when we ask for help and fail, we can shift our strategy over and over again until we meet our need. This means we escape overwhelm currents, find relief, and also naturally discover our true gifts and talents, which add meaning to our life.

A PERSONAL EXAMPLE OF THE ULTIMATE EMPOWERING THOUGHT

Those of us who have been trapped in the Ultimate Overwhelming Thought are likely cling to certain labels of ourselves for too long, denying ourselves the opportunity to find our true talents. For example, I labeled myself a computer programmer for five years because I thought that being a programmer would bring me success and therefore meet my need for financial security and happiness. But lo and behold, after implementing the H.E.L.P. method, I found my success as an author and entrepreneur! I had the courage to switch my label because I learned to think the Ultimate Empowering Thought.

Publishing this book is the pinnacle of my career so far. It's my name on the cover. It's my thoughts in the book. It sure looks like an individual achievement. But it isn't, not at all. This book, which is both a large accomplishment and an extremely meaningful piece of work to me personally, is a result of getting help.

While publishing this book, I asked for every bit of help I could find. Here are a few ways I did so:

- I asked dozens of friends to read drafts and give feedback.
- I hired an editor to edit both the content and the grammar of the book.
- I hired an artist to create my book cover.
- I reached out to every single willing friend and family member to help me promote the book.
- I sought help from multiple therapists to manage my anxiety so that I could write.
- I attended an online support group for writers where we wrote together. In fact, almost the entirety of this book was composed while on a Zoom meeting with other writers for moral support.
- Oh, and I also was financially dependent on my wife for the entirety of the time I was writing.

In addition to asking for help, I also used the other component of the Ultimate Empowering Thought: I tried as many times as I needed until I was successful. I started writing on a blog site in 2016, over six years before I published this book. I created numerous coaching programs and written products that failed to gain traction. I wrote a full ebook on digital detoxing and published it, only to sell a handful of copies for ninety-nine cents and one copy for ten dollars to my mom (thanks, Mom!). When writing *Help! I'm Overwhelmed!*, I rewrote three entire drafts from scratch until I settled on this fourth draft of the manuscript. Had I been graded by the standard school system, my efforts to find entrepreneurial success would have been lower than F—I wasn't even close to being half successful!

Yet I kept trying, and now you hold this book in your hands because I held onto the Ultimate Empowering

Thought: I knew that I could try as many times as I wanted to meet my need (helping people live better lives and connecting with them over that common interest), and ultimately I have. I didn't do it on the first try, and I certainly didn't do it alone. I did it with H.E.L.P. Whether my book is an "A+" book or whether it's written in the "right" way isn't important—what's important is that it helps you be less overwhelmed, which meets your need (being less overwhelmed) and my need (helping people).

Self-sufficiency is a myth. We don't birth ourselves. We don't raise ourselves. We don't teach ourselves. Every step of the way, we need the help of others. School and work try to teach us that we are individuals, products of only our own will and achievements, but this is a lie.

Perfection is also a myth. Life is chaotic, and things are always changing, so even if we get a perfect grade on something, we're sure to face another challenge where we're not good enough. As ancient Greek philosopher Heraclitus famously said, "Nothing endures but change." Things can never be perfect if they are always changing.

Choose to let go of the Ultimate Overwhelming Thought that you need to be perfect on the first try by yourself, and instead choose to believe the Ultimate Empowering Thought: you can try as many times as you want, with as much help as you can find, until you meet your need.

CHAPTER FOUR

H IS FOR HALT THE PANIC

I n this chapter we'll dive into detail on how we need to start our H.E.L.P. process by halting our panic. First, we need to pick something specific that's overwhelming us.

WHAT'S OVERWHELMING YOU?

School and work have trained you into accepting a state of overwhelm, which can affect all areas of your life. In fact, you're probably feeling stressed, burnt out, and anxious thanks to a whole host of factors. Separately or together, these factors—these currents threatening to drag you under—attack your sense of peace. Here are some ways that your overwhelm might be manifesting:

- **You feel disoriented in a certain situation.** For example, at work you receive so many emails that you can barely keep track of them all without your head spinning.

- **You feel like you're not making any progress no matter how hard you try.** For example, you keep trying new organizational methods to keep your house clean, but no matter how many cleaning videos you watch on YouTube, you can't seem to keep your house from turning into a mess.
- **You have the sense that life is just too much and feel resentful or frustrated.** For example, your baby is up all night crying, and the next day you resent any minor inconvenience because you don't have the energy to cope with everyday life.

Since it's impossible to tackle all your overwhelm at once, this book asks you to choose just one current of overwhelm and work through it with the H.E.L.P. method. I recommend beginning with just one overwhelming problem because this process is about building momentum. Each time you walk through H.E.L.P. with a different overwhelming problem, you'll get better and better at it! So while it's tempting to list every single way you're overwhelmed right now, I'll ask you to stick to one.

Maybe there's something big weighing on you, screaming to be addressed. That's a great place to start! Or, if starting with something huge seems too scary, then maybe there's something small but obvious you're procrastinating. You can use the H.E.L.P. method on that. You can pick an overwhelming thing from any area of life: career, relationship, physical or mental health, home, etc. If you're overwhelmed, it counts!

At this point, fill out the portion of the H.E.L.P. worksheet shown below. This is the worksheet's first line, and that focus will let you prioritize your energies on tackling this single overwhelm current. You'll add a little more to your H.E.L.P. worksheet with each chapter you read.

I am overwhelmed by: _____

THE DIFFERENT FACES OF PANIC

The next step is to recognize the ways you panic in response to your overwhelm. The first thing swimmers are taught about rip currents is to stop panicking. According to *Merriam-Webster*, panic is "a sudden unreasoning terror often accompanied by mass flight." The key thing to notice is that panic is "unreasoning"—if someone is panicking, they're behaving in such a way as to cause a negative consequence, not a positive one.

For a swimmer in a rip current, panic behavior looks like swimming toward the shore even though they can't outswim the current. With each terrified stroke, the swimmer thinks they're making progress, when really they're exhausting themselves and going nowhere.

For a person in an overwhelm current, panic looks different but follows the same principles as swimming against the current:

- It is guaranteed to fail in the long term, because the force being panicked against is stronger than the individual panicking.
- It creates a net negative effect; it drains energy from the individual panicking and puts chaos into the environment, so while they may make some small amount of progress in the short term, the panicker will make things worse in the long run.

- It creates a false feeling of progress. Because panicking feels like a lot of work, we become obsessed and keep panicking, thinking that just one more bit of panicking will do the trick. Unfortunately, it never does, so we remain trapped in a cycle of false progress.

One other dangerous attribute of panic is that it grows quickly internally and spreads quickly between people. *Merriam-Webster* says that panic is often "accompanied by mass flight." I personally prefer the term "mass hysteria." When we panic, we spread that panic to others, who then spread it to more people, and soon all people are panicking, to the detriment of everyone. When we spiral into panic, panic then spirals out of our control.

The implication of this is that when you try to stop panicking, you'll still be surrounded by others who are spreading panic among themselves and to you. It will be tempting to give in and think, "Well, if so-and-so says this panic behavior is ok, then I should also be doing this!" But remember: most people are overwhelmed, and most overwhelmed people are panicking people. You don't want to keep doing what they're doing!

When in doubt, evaluate whether a person is operating by the Ultimate Overwhelming Thought ("I should be able to do this perfectly the first time, by myself, but I can't, so I am a failure") or the Ultimate Empowering Thought ("I can try this thing as many times as I want, with as much help as I can find, until I find a way to meet my needs"), and only take their advice if they're operating from empowerment.

In my experience, panic behaviors generally fall into one of four main categories: fighting/creating conflict, people pleasing, self-criticism, and perfectionism.

Fighting/Creating Conflict

At the core, fighting or creating conflict is a panic behavior because it creates a net negative result; even if the problem is "solved," additional overwhelm ends up entering the environment from the friction of the fight.

Think about the last time you got furious at someone and yelled at them. You probably felt that you were in the right and that they had wronged you somehow, so you let your anger out and yelled to express your feelings. There are two ways this could have played out. First, the other person might have yelled back at you. You may have entered into a blow-up fight, which caused pain to both sides and didn't resolve the problem. Clearly, this result is not favorable. From the swimmer trapped in the rip current's perspective, it's like fighting the current and drowning faster.

But what if your fighting worked? What if by yelling, you caused the other person to stop their behavior and act how you wanted? In this scenario, the "solution" you've created by fighting is only temporary. Chances are the person you yelled at harbored resentment. They might have started to pick more fights with you later, or if you were more powerful than them, they might have started to exhibit passive-aggressive behaviors that harmed you. Perhaps they refused to help you when you needed a hand. Ultimately, the long-term result of you yelling at someone is probably more overwhelm, not less. From the rip current perspective, this is like making progress against the current for a few seconds, only to be overwhelmed and sucked right back out.

For another take on why fighting is so harmful, consider how fighting operates in nature among animals. I recently saw a nature documentary on predators in the wild, and it informed me that predators rarely fight with each other over territory. I watched an altercation between two jaguars. They tussled for a moment over territory, but then one jaguar claimed the upper hand and sent the other skittering off. These jaguars didn't fight to the death because they knew that even the winning jaguar would become weakened and vulnerable.

When we fight or create conflict, whether physically or with words, we're subject to the same law: even the winner of the fight is harmed by the act of fighting.

When you're overwhelmed, it's tempting to fight back to secure more space for yourself. Instead, I encourage you to exercise nature's other option: flight. If you're angry at someone, instead of fighting with them, set a boundary and take space for yourself to rest and recover. If you're being unfairly attacked by someone, remove yourself from the situation and recruit allies to help you out. Then, once you've calmed down and can communicate and/or stand up for yourself without panicking, do so in the appropriate manner.

When we fight in the heat of the moment, we create conflict, increasing our overwhelm. When we step away, cool down, and handle things calmly at a later time, we resolve conflict, reducing our overwhelm.

PEOPLE PLEASING

People pleasing creates the same sense of false progress that fighting does. When I was in an overwhelming corporate work situation, I would often spend hours agonizing over my emails. I was so worried that I'd send something wrong, or leave someone off, or make a grammatical error.

This behavior was classic people pleasing, which I define as obsessively focusing on pleasing someone to the exclusion of all other values or objectives. The reason people pleasing is always an unhelpful panic behavior is because it's impossible to guarantee that you'll please all the people in your life, so if you obsessively focus on doing that, you'll not only fail to please everyone, you'll also let everything else in your life fall apart.

I also frequently sat at my computer, scared to take a walk or a break, because I was worried what would happen if someone messaged me right when I had left. In essence, I worried that if I didn't perform appropriately, other people would be displeased. I figured that because I was already experiencing overwhelm, the best way to make myself feel better was to please as many people as possible until the overwhelm went away. People pleasing seemed like a way to manage a situation that felt totally unmanageable.

My people pleasing behavior didn't only take place at work. To please Preetha, I constantly attended social outings that I didn't want to go to. To please my professors in college, I worked harder and longer to make my answers to assignments perfect. People pleasing used to be rampant in my life, and I never questioned it simply because I was too panicked. I didn't know there was another option, so I swam as hard as I could against the current even though I was going nowhere.

People pleasing hurt instead of helping because I was so obsessed with keeping people from being mad at me that I ended up letting the rest of my life fall to pieces, which ultimately harmed both myself and others. Worrying about my emails at work gave me anxiety and heartburn, which led me to get medical procedures to test my stomach and heart even though they were fine. Going to social events I didn't have the energy for with Preetha caused me to pick blow-up fights with her, thus furthering the panic spiral I was in. And remember how panic spreads? My arguments with Preetha caused her to panic in response as she retaliated in our fights. The professors whom I constantly worried about pleasing? Their lives weren't changed by my grades! They respected me regardless of how my assignments turned out. All my people pleasing was harmful to myself and others while resolving nothing.

As with all panic behaviors, the key to stopping people pleasing is to see that it is harmful, and that the feeling of progress it creates is a lie.

SELF-CRITICISM BASED ON THE ULTIMATE OVERWHELMING THOUGHT

The third type of panic behavior to stop doing is criticizing yourself based on the Ultimate Overwhelming Thought. Let's kick off our examination of this panic behavior with a humorous example involving tennis. I played competitive tennis throughout my childhood, and let me assure you that tennis players are notorious self-critics. Once you're alone on that court for long enough, you start to go a little bit nuts and say all kinds of things to yourself!

I had one friend on the college tennis team who was particularly self-critical. He was an excellent player, but when he was losing, he was a spectacle to watch. He'd miss a shot and yell to himself, "Are you *kidding me*?! A *six-year-old* could have made that shot!" Or, after failing to reach a ball that the opponent hit, he might yell, "You're *slower* than an *old grandpa* out here!"

In this scenario, it was clear to anyone watching that my friend was perhaps a little bit crazy when it came to the self-criticism. After all, was yelling at himself going to help him win his match? Clearly not, because the more he yelled, the worse he played. He was fighting himself and losing. It would have been much better for him to remain calm and focus his energy on what he wanted to achieve, such as running faster or hitting the ball in the court. He'd have been much better saying to himself, "Focus on the ball, you can do it!" And yet he chose to use his energy to criticize himself pointlessly.

The reason my friend's criticism was pointless and harmful wasn't because all criticism is bad—it was because of the implicit assumption underneath his criticisms. In his mind, he *should have been able to* make the shot that a "six-year-old could have made." He *should have been able to* run faster to get to the ball instead of running "slower than an old grandpa." Underneath his statement was our dear nemesis the Ultimate Overwhelming Thought!

Self-criticism is often an irrational, panicked way of pretending to improve by labeling ourselves failures or saying we should do better. Like creating conflict and people pleasing, this type of self-criticism doesn't help us improve at all.

You probably have a constant internal dialogue, some of which is filled with critical thoughts toward yourself. You might think, "I'm fat. I need to lose thirty pounds to be at my perfect weight," or "I'm no good at my job. I'm a failure," or "I should be doing a better job at writing this book right now" (okay, maybe that one is personal to me). I believe that even the mildest form of self-criticism, such as telling myself I should be doing better at writing my book, is a panic behavior that is harming me *if it contains an underlying assumption from the Ultimate Overwhelming Thought.*

Notice that all those example criticisms contained either "perfect," "failure," or "should be." These superlative phrases are all signs that your thought is not a helpful criticism but instead a sneaky version of the Ultimate Overwhelming Thought.

When is criticism helpful? It's helpful when it aligns with the Ultimate Empowering Thought!

If you feel you're overeating, you might say, "I notice my body is asking for healthier food. I can try to get help with eating healthier so that I meet my need of being active and healthy!" If you're struggling at work, you might say, "I'm not completing my assignments on time. I can try to work faster with a new method. If that doesn't work, I can try something else! I'm sure I can find a way to meet my need of getting my work done on time if I keep trying."

If you're having difficulty writing a book (like me), you might say, "Wow, writing a book is hard! My ideas aren't as clear as I want them to be. I can try to write with more clarity and purpose, but I'll need help! I can hire an editor to help me refine my ideas" (which I did!).

As you can see, the key words that make criticism helpful are "can try," "keep trying," "meet my need," "help," and other empowering words. Notice that criticisms that come from empowerment tend to state the facts rather than dramatize the problem. In these examples, the criticism noticed that the body was asking for healthier food, the work assignments weren't getting completed, and the ideas weren't as clear as desired. These are still criticisms, but they are stated as facts, with empowering suggestions for finding solutions attached, all based on meeting a genuine need.

Lay down your self-criticisms that come from overwhelm and empower yourself instead!

PERFECTIONISM

Perfectionism is a panic behavior that I think results from the school and corporate measurement systems addressed in chapter three. After all, we've been taught that at both school and work, nothing is ever good enough, so we need to make things perfect. I define perfectionism as trying to improve something because you can't stop thinking about how it is flawed, which causes you to lose sight of the bigger picture. For example, in school, I could never stop thinking about the test questions that I missed, even when I got an A on a test. And the time I spent worrying about tests led me to fail to see the bigger picture of taking care of my mental health. This resulted in a full-scale depressive episode. For my tennis teammate, his desire to be perfect on the court led him to endless self-criticism.

Perfectionism is generally marked by thinking that "just one more bit" will be enough, like when you're fixing your hair to go out and think, "If I could just get this one hair into place!" The truth is most people won't notice your one hair sticking out. And if they do, does it matter? In the grand scheme of things, of course not.

Perfectionism is also marked by a lack of gratitude for how good life is. When you're in the perfectionist zone, you tend to be so homed in on the fact that something is imperfect that you fail to see how great parts of your life are in general. When I was in my perfectionist spiral in school, I failed to appreciate that I had supportive friends, loving family, and an amazing life. Instead, I became depressed because the only thing I could think about was missing test questions.

I'm a broken record at this point, but as with all the other panic behaviors, perfectionism creates a false sense of progress. If you pick some small detail and let it consume your mind, then you feel as if you have control. You may be totally overwhelmed and drowning in the rip current of life, but if you can picture how you're going to perfect this teeny-tiny thing, then you feel some small sense of relief. Sadly, as the pressure of life's overwhelming challenges builds, you'll eventually end up drowning anyway regardless of whether you perfect things.

TAKING YOUR PANIC INVENTORY

Now that we've covered some of the main types of panic actions, it's time for you to take your own panic inventory on your H.E.L.P. worksheet. Write down all the ways you panic in response to the problem that's overwhelming you.

The next step is to admit that you're really in an overwhelm current that's stronger than you, and that your panic behaviors aren't helping at all.

It can be scary to admit that what you're doing to fight your current isn't working. The good news is that help is going to come with new solutions and possibilities that you never knew were possible! At this time, the most important thing is that you become aware of all the ways you're panicking. You don't even have to fully stop your panic behaviors right now—you just need to accept that your panic behaviors aren't working.

Notice that I've left a section marked "other" on the panic behaviors list. That's because any action that meets the panic criteria I described (fails in the long term, drains your energy, creates a false sense of progress) can be a panic behavior. Feel free to reflect on whether you use any other behaviors to panic against your overwhelm and write them in the "other" space.

At this point, fill out the portion of the H.E.L.P. worksheet shown below.

I panic in these ways:

• Fighting/creating conflict: _____

• People pleasing: _____

• Overwhelm-based criticism: _____

• Perfectionism: _____

• Other panic behaviors: _____

I, _____, accept that _____ (the overwhelm from line one) is an overwhelm current that is stronger than me. I am fully willing to give up these panic behaviors and accept help.

If you chose to fill out that last statement, congratulations! You are now entitled to your first big wave of relief, which is the reward of the H.E.L.P. method. Look at those panic behaviors that you wrote out. Realize that you never have to force yourself to do these things again! How amazing is that? You may still find yourself doing them by instinct, and that's okay. Just gently remind yourself that you no longer believe in these behaviors.

You may feel embarrassed that you have been doing so many useless, stressful behaviors. That's totally fine as well! One thing I like to remember is that usually the only one who believed that my panic behaviors were working was me. So when I admit that my panic behaviors aren't necessary anymore, it's not like the world suddenly sees my admission. They probably already knew that I was in a state of panic. Or, more likely, everyone's probably so busy with their own panic behaviors that they didn't even notice my change. Embarrassment is fine to feel; know that it will pass.

Finally, realize that just by being aware of your panic behaviors, you have the first piece of a *lasting* solution that brings relief. Once you see your people-pleasing emails, or your self-critical inner talk, or your emotional blow-ups as the useless behaviors they are, you don't ever have to go back to unseeing them. Without forcing yourself to do a single thing differently, you will become happier and more relieved because you will naturally perform fewer of these panic behaviors.

Take a deep breath, and settle into that wonderful feeling of freedom that comes from admitting you can't do it all. You're on your way to a more peaceful and meaningful life already!

CHAPTER FIVE

E IS FOR ENGAGE EMOTIONS

Our rip current analogy has been a useful tool up until this point, but you may still doubt it. Namely, you may wonder if the consequences of not asking for help are truly death like they are for the swimmer who panics. That's a fair question. After all, you're alive and reading this book— you've survived this long. My answer to this question is that while you may not have died from your overwhelm currents, you are very likely to be drowning in many areas. You're just drowning your emotions instead of your physical body.

I define "drowning your emotions" as seeking out excessive physical or mental stimulation in order to distract oneself from one's emotions, which come from overwhelm.

Here's how I think drowning our emotions works. We feel overwhelmed, and our panic behaviors aren't working. We don't like the many emotions that come with feeling overwhelmed. We may feel angry, sad, resentful, confused, afraid, and ashamed. If we were to sit still and meditate, we'd have to feel all these feelings, and we're afraid to do so because we know they'll hurt, so instead we drown our emotions with a stimulating activity. We may drink too much alcohol, play too many video games, or work more than we should in order to avoid having to simply sit and feel. At the end of the day, if we're seeking excessive stimulation to avoid feeling our emotions, we're drowning them!

Drowning our emotions is harmful because while it helps us hide from our overwhelm in the short term, it makes us significantly more overwhelmed in the long term. The longer we repress or avoid our emotions, the more they build up inside. In order to avoid the building emotions, we resort to further drowning behaviors—more drinking, more video games, more workaholism. This leads us into a cycle of increasing overwhelm, which worsens the negative symptoms of overwhelm.

In this way, drowning emotions is a lot like panicking: it distracts us from being overwhelmed in the short term, but it always causes significant harm in the long term. The difference between panicking and drowning emotions is that when we panic, we try to fight our overwhelm head on, on our own. When we drown our emotions, we try to hide from our overwhelm and pretend it isn't there. Neither method of avoiding overwhelm works!

I believe we drown our emotions through three major behavioral categories: excessive physical pleasure (drugs, alcohol, food, etc.), uncontrolled screen time (phone, TV, computer, etc.), and obsessive busyness (workaholism, obsessively helping others, etc.).

EXCESSIVE PHYSICAL PLEASURE

I define seeking excessive physical pleasure as doing a practice that feels pleasurable to your body now but has negative health consequences for your body in the long term. For example, consider the person who drinks too much alcohol. They feel good in the moment, but in the morning, they have a hangover. Consider the hard drug user—they get high now but must deal with addiction and withdrawal later. The National Center for Drug Abuse Statistics says that 19.4 percent of people in the US have used illicit drugs or misused prescription drugs *within the past year*. (https://drugabus-estatistics.org/)

Before you let yourself off easy for not abusing hard drugs illegally, be honest with yourself about whether you ever use cigarettes, alcohol, or recreational marijuana to drown your emotions.

If we count cigarettes and alcohol as drugs, then 60.2 percent of Americans aged twelve and over are currently abusing drugs, meaning they have used in the past thirty days.

Take a moment and consider why you use these substances. Regardless of their health impact, these drugs are dangerous because they provide an easy, socially acceptable way to drown emotions.

Having a rough week at work? Go to the bar and drink it off.

Stressed about family issues? Go outside and have a smoke.

Worried about money? Pop a pill.

Taking drugs is not the only form of seeking excessive physical pleasure, however. Any pleasurable thing that causes harm later falls into this category. Another behavior that affects a large portion of the population is using food to drown emotions. Have you ever been stressed and just wanted to eat something sweet to feel better? Have you ever been exhausted and overwhelmed and devoured a bag of chips while watching TV?

If you've done these things, then you've drowned your emotions using food. And there are consequences for this eating just like with drugs, since you're eating more food than your body needs or eating foods that bring you low energy and headaches.

I'm not judging you for these behaviors. In fact, the only reason I know so much about them is because I've done so many of them myself! I've drowned emotions through food and alcohol more times than I can count. In the moment, distracting myself with physical pleasure makes me forget my overwhelm and ignore my feelings of anger, frustration, sadness, and anxiety. Enjoying the physical sensation of a drink or that bag of chips means I'm not experiencing the hurt my emotions are sure to bring.

EXCESSIVE SCREEN TIME

While you may be somewhat on your guard against the ill effects of seeking physical pleasure through drugs or food, you're probably also drowning your emotions with something more insidious—excessive screen time. I consider drowning through excessive screen time to be when you're using any type of technology to escape the world or your emotions due to overwhelm. While physical pleasure is all about enjoying the moment, screen time allows us to totally zone out.

Screen time is far more socially acceptable than drugs, it's less effort to access at a moment's notice, and it's easier to sustain with fewer immediate physical aftereffects. Yet I believe that when we use screen time excessively, we enforce the same panic and drowning patterns that we do when we use drugs.

I believe screen time became the most dangerous form of drowning emotions after the rise of smartphones and the invention of the newsfeed. In the past, we accessed social media sites like Facebook or Myspace on a computer and visited people's pages or walls. When I was in elementary school, I would get on my computer, log in to Myspace, and then decide which friends' pages I wanted to explore. I would do this for some finite period of time, then I would move on to other things.

Now when I get on social media, I can access it right from my phone. The first thing I see isn't someone's wall—it's a newsfeed that compiles everyone's updates into one unending stream. Because of this, I can scroll for as long as I want without noticing time passing. There are no stopping cues to make me pause and take a break. I keep going and going until I can pull myself away. The result is that I end up browsing this feed for longer than I wanted to—for an excessive amount of time.

The same principles apply to streaming television. In the past, you had a scheduled program, and when it was over you stopped. Now most people watch television on streaming services like Netflix. When watching a show on Netflix, one episode ends, and the next episode automatically begins after a measly five seconds. There is no time to think about whether you want to watch the next episode—you're already watching it!

Doing just one of these behaviors is enough to drown your emotions, but let's be honest: how long has it been since you watched TV while scrolling social media on your phone at the same time? I think it's safe to assume that it hasn't been that long since this has happened to you. These days, it's not just the content of television or Instagram that turns you into a bingeing zombie; screen time's permanent availability lets you be a zombie without an end in sight.

The final factor that makes excessive screen time the most dangerous drowning behavior is that it's socially encouraged and acceptable. When I was trapped in overwhelm and spending all my time drowning my emotions by watching video games on streaming channels, I noticed that I received both ads to stop smoking and ads to start playing more video games. While smoking is generally discouraged by society, gaming is encouraged far more regularly. Video games often advertise themselves as "the most addictive game of the year." "Addictive" is a word they use positively! This is mind-blowing, considering millions of people suffer from addiction.

Or consider television. What do you think when you hear the phrase "Netflix binge"? You probably think, "Yep, that's something I do now and then." After browsing my TV's streaming channels, I found that at least three streaming services specifically had a category named "bingeworthy." If I'm at a social gathering and there's nothing to talk about, I might say, "What TV shows have you binged lately?" When bingeing is involved with alcohol or food, it's considered a life-threatening behavior. When bingeing is involved with streaming services, it's a socially encouraged hobby.

It's probably true that bingeing Netflix every day is less likely to kill you in the short term than eating five Big Macs in a row or drinking twelve beers daily. But bingeing on social media, video games, television, or any other type of screen time is no different than using drugs or food when it comes to drowning emotions and escaping from reality. If anything, it's drugs 2.0! The overconsumption of escapism feels better than painful emotions. However, the emotions of your overwhelm demand to be heard, no matter how long you scroll on your phone. Bingeing on anything is never healthy.

OBSESSIVE BUSYNESS

I'm willing to bet that the majority of people use addictive pleasure and screen time to drown their emotions. But if you don't use either of those things too much, then I suspect you have a logical reason why—you're too busy!

The simplest way you may stay busy to drown your emotions is by overworking. As a life coach, I often help people make career transitions or decide new career goals. There's one type of client harder to help than any other: the person working eighty hours a week at a job they hate. This person is not only panicking against a job they don't like, they've given up hope at change and submerged themselves in the work so that they don't have to think about anything else. I have immense grace and love for this person, but I know that I can rarely help them until they admit that they're using obsessive overworking to avoid their emotions.

Another way to stay busy is to be obsessive about helping others. You may not overwork at your job, but you may have far too many people who depend on you at home. You may constantly be running errands for this friend, or that nonprofit, or that church group. Unfortunately, doing these good things can be a way of drowning if it's done obsessively to avoid dealing with your own emotions.

As you can see, drowning doesn't have anything to do with what society says about an activity. It's about what it does to you by helping you avoid your overwhelm. After all, drugs are generally considered bad by society, screen time is generally considered neutral, and work and helping others are generally considered good. Yet all of these activities are equally capable of letting a person escape from their emotions, and all can be done in excess.

To get help, you must take an honest look at all three categories of behavior and see the ways you're drowning your emotions, regardless of what society thinks about the behavior.

HOW TO TELL DROWNING EMOTIONS BEHAVIORS FROM ACCEPTABLE EVERYDAY ACTIVITIES

I've made a pretty strong case that physical pleasure, screen time, and busyness are dangerous because they can let you drown your emotions, which harms you. But these things are all part of everyday life; how do we know whether we're using them in an acceptable manner or whether we're drowning our emotions and avoiding our problems? Must we quit every single possible pleasurable behavior and become monks in order to stop drowning our emotions? I don't think so.

Instead, I think we should measure each possible drowning behavior against the two criteria from the definition of drowning emotions (seeking excessive stimulation to avoid feeling our emotions). First, is it *excessive* stimulation? *Merriam-Webster* defines bingeing as "an unrestrained and often excessive indulgence," so bingeing is an example of something that's always a drowning behavior, because it is by definition excessive. Whether it's with food, alcohol, or television, bingeing is drowning your emotions.

Another example of excessive stimulation would be taking illegal drugs or misusing prescription drugs. Drugs like cocaine, heroin, and methamphetamine provide excessive stimulation to the brain, causing a variety of horrific symptoms and leading to addiction. The same is true of misusing prescription drugs. We can easily say that using drugs in this way is drowning emotions, since the physical stimulation these drugs provide is always unhealthily excessive.

The second criteria from my definition of drowning emotions is to "avoid feeling our emotions." It's hard to be self-aware of when I'm avoiding my emotions, so instead I measure something correlated with feeling my emotions: making genuine connection with other human beings. Chances are, if I'm genuinely connecting with someone, I'm not drowning my emotions. And chances are, if I'm doing a potential drowning behavior alone in isolation, then I am in fact drowning my emotions.

Consider an adult of legal drinking age who consumes alcohol. They may go to the local bar with a group of friends, have two beers, and talk about a variety of deep and emotional topics. Compare this to a person who goes home, grabs two beers from the fridge, and zones out to a TV show while their friends go out without them. In this scenario, it's likely that the social drinker is engaging their emotions, while the isolated drinker is drowning them.

The same can be true for work and screen time. If you're working seventy hours a week alone in your basement, you're probably drowning your emotions. If you're working seventy hours a week on an intense, collaborative project, achieving something meaningful with your coworkers, you may be engaging your emotions.

I believe the simplest possible way to minimize emotional drowning with the behaviors listed above is by using a rule of thumb I call "two, together." This means no more than two indulgences of the given behavior, and only done with someone you emotionally connect with.

I created this rule based on troublesome patterns in my own TV watching. Preetha and I used to binge television frequently, often watching four or more episodes in a row. I noticed that by the third episode, I wasn't enjoying it anymore—it began to feel excessive. It seemed that two episodes was a good number for me. I also noticed that whenever I watched TV alone, I immediately felt worse, even if I only watched one episode! When I found myself alone, it was much better to rest, read, meditate, or do something fulfilling, as just a single episode felt either excessive or an escape from my emotions.

However, when Preetha and I watched two episodes together, I had an awesome time. We'd pause the show and talk about what we thought would happen. And because our TV time was limited, we'd take the chance beforehand to go to the park with our dog, Willie. In other words, we were making a genuine connection during just a short viewing. By setting the boundary of "two, together," I've been able to significantly cut down on my drowning with TV.

If you live alone, you can still use the rule of "two, together" by seeking out friends with the same interests as you, or by FaceTiming a friend while you do something together. When I was working an extra two hours a day to write the key parts of this book, I joined an impromptu Zoom meeting with friends where we all worked on projects together. When I want to watch TV but I'm alone, I'll find a friend who I can FaceTime while we watch the same show at the same time!

By doing this, we maintain a social bond and engage our emotions, even though we're in separate physical places. "Two, together" is possible even if you live alone!

"Two, together" is a handy rule because it accommodates your desire to engage in pleasurable behaviors while taking away their power to drown you. Whether it's two beers (for legal-drinking-age adults, of course), two episodes, or two extra hours working, if you do it with someone else in a socially engaged way, you'll be using those behaviors not to drown your emotions but to engage them—the subject of our next section.

WHY ENGAGING YOUR EMOTIONS IS WORTH IT

After you stop drowning your emotions as much, you're going to start feeling them. This will probably be a strange, new experience! You'll also probably be afraid that your emotions are going to hurt you or make you hurt others. In this section I want to show you that engaging your emotions is worth the temporary pain of feeling them because your emotions are valuable tools that increase your quality of life, and because over time engaging your emotions will feel good even as it hurts.

When I say, "engage emotions," what I mean is seeking contact with your emotions instead of pushing them away. It means truly feeling what you're feeling. When you engage with someone in conversation, you walk up, talk, and listen. I think you can do the same with your emotions—you can seek them out and try to hear what they're saying. Ultimately, a person with engaged emotions is a person who knows what their emotions are communicating to them. When you have a pit in your stomach or a warmth in your chest, you'll be able to interpret what those physical feelings mean. And you'll learn to pay attention to, and label, your emotions; instead of the default response of "I'm fine," you'll recognize when you're angry, or grieving, or hopeful, and on and on. Engaging your emotions simply means starting this conversation with them and seeking to understand them over time.

Let's open ourselves to the possibility of engaging our emotions more by the example of engaging with joy. Joy is generally considered positive. Imagine the joy a parent feels when they see their child happy and healthy. That's an amazing feeling! Imagine the joy you feel when you're doing your favorite hobby. That's an amazing feeling too! Joy is something worth engaging, so it's a good place to start. When you drown your emotions less, you'll be able to feel more of this amazing joy, which is awesome!

But what about other so-called negative emotions like sadness, anger, and fear? If we open up to joy, don't we open up to these too? I think we do. My experience has been that if I drown my emotions, I drown them all at once. If I choose to engage my emotions, I have to engage them all at once. Imagine someone numbed your hand with an anesthetic. You wouldn't feel the burn of a hot pan, but you also wouldn't feel the gentle caress of your partner's touch. Numbness takes away both sensations, regardless of whether we consider them good or bad. I think the same principles apply to our emotions when we numb them through drowning behaviors.

Is it worth it to engage with all the "negative" emotions like sadness, anger, and fear in order to feel positive emotions like joy and love? Absolutely! Consider this: given the option, would you voluntarily choose to live your life with a permanently numb hand so that you never felt pain, or would you rather keep living with a hand that can feel? My answer is easy—I'd rather keep my feeling! This isn't just because I think the pleasure of a caress outweighs the pain of a hot pan; it's also because the feeling in my hand gives me information about the world that helps me take the right action. If I couldn't feel my hand and I accidentally set it on a hot countertop, I might burn myself severely. If my hand was numb, I'd struggle to tie shoes, hold a pencil, type on a keyboard, and drive a car.

When we choose to numb ourselves, whether physically or emotionally, we're committing a self-harm behavior that squanders some of our precious gifts. It is not the physical or emotional disability that's harming us—it's our choice to take something that we were gifted with and numb it out on purpose that reduces our quality of life. Our unique gifts are valuable and we should engage them all!

Feeling emotions is valuable for the exact same reason as feeling our hands. When we feel our emotions, we get information about what our body wants us to do, which keeps us safe and increases our quality of life. Feeling fear tells us to flee from a scenario that is harmful. Feeling anger tells us to stand up for ourselves or to set a healthy boundary with someone. Feeling sadness tells us to recognize what we've lost and to be at peace. Feeling our emotions is just as helpful as feeling our limbs!

This may not be your typical experience with emotions. You may think that anger makes you hurt people, fear makes you isolate yourself, and sadness makes you depressed. What gives? When your emotions seem to make you act unhelpfully, it's because they're extreme emotions created in a state of overwhelm. For example, if as a child your alcoholic father yelled and threw things at you, then you probably learned that fear and anger were very scary things. If people you grew up with had chronic depression, you might feel that sadness only makes things worse.

I have good news: by seeking help and by escaping your overwhelm, you can start to use your emotions—all of them!—as amazing, helpful tools. You'll be able to slowly let go of these extreme emotions created in a state of overwhelm. You'll be able to use sadness, fear, and anger as tools to make your life better. And amazingly, feeling sadness, fear, and anger will even start to feel good sometimes.

For a quick example of how engaging with a negative emotion can feel good, let's consider a personal experience I had with sadness. In the summer of 2021, I was forced to rehome a puppy I'd adopted. Daphne was a beautiful, sweet puppy, but she was unmanageably aggressive toward my other pup. Feeling that I had failed Daphne—and having to go through the agonizing process of finding her a new home—left me feeling overwhelmed. Luckily, after a couple months of interviewing, I found her an amazing family who loves her very much and can keep her feeling safe.

In the immediate aftermath of rehoming Daphne, I simply felt relief from being overwhelmed. But one day as I was running errands, the song "Happier" by Marshmello and Bastille came on the radio. It's a song about splitting up with someone because it's for the best. Because I was going through just this process with Daphne, I felt a large swell of sadness in my chest. But, like many of us, I thought that feeling more sadness in the moment would only make me feel worse overall. Daphne was already gone—what was the point of grieving? Wouldn't it make the hurt more acute? So I changed the station and ignored my sadness.

Later, as I arrived home from my final errand, "Happier" once again started playing. I thought that perhaps this coincidence was too important to ignore, so I left the song on and engaged my sadness. I pulled into the garage and cried. I didn't cry just a little—I cried heaving, sobbing, snotty, ugly cries. I had a full-blown catharsis, which is when a bunch of previously drowned emotions get released.

Afterwards, I realized something startling.

Not only had it felt good to cry, but I felt an enormous sense of *relief* after expressing the sadness I had been holding in, and the sadness itself dissipated. It seemed that by engaging with my emotions, I could find relief from my emotional overwhelm.

I now believe this to be true about almost all emotions. If we drown our emotions, we live a life of numbness that severely limits not just our ability to feel good but also our ability to accomplish things and be functional. Plus, we can only drown our emotions so far before we have an emotional outburst and hurt ourselves or others. And these outbursts make us even more afraid of our emotions, which makes us drown them even more, which leads to worse outbursts when we lose control! It's a never-ending cycle!

If we instead choose to engage our emotions, we feel a burst of pain as they come up, but we also feel the relief of processing them and experience a massive boost of functionality in our lives because we have the guidance of our emotions.

And the more we learn to engage with our emotions, and the more progress we make toward getting help with our overwhelm, the less we have extreme emotional reactions that are harmful. By far, one of the biggest benefits of using the H.E.L.P. method in my own life is that because I have so much help, I feel like my emotions are my ally. They are fun to engage with, and they are also a secret weapon that helps me succeed in life.

You can have this weapon too should you engage your emotions!

At this point, fill out the portion of the H.E.L.P. worksheet shown below.

I use the following activities to drown my emotions:

Physical pleasure: _____

Screen time: _____

Busyness: _____

I, _____, accept that I have been drowning my emotions. I accept that the drowning behaviors listed above are harmful. I believe that my emotions are there to help me. I'm willing to engage them.

CHAPTER SIX

L IS FOR LOOK FOR HELP

I hope that by now, the reason *why* you should ask for help is clear. Society's systems like work and school make us overwhelmed, causing mental health challenges that make us feel like we're drowning. Overwhelmed and lacking help, we resort to panic behaviors, and when those fail, we drown our emotions and exist in a state of constant overwhelm, often suffering negative health consequences as a result. Just like a swimmer trapped in a rip current, we are trapped in overwhelm currents, and we *must receive external help in order to escape these overwhelm currents.* There is no other option, because overwhelm currents are too big to fight on our own.

In this chapter, we'll address the *what* and the *how* of looking for help. We'll start by examining the very first barrier to getting help, something I call the "overwhelm checkmate," and how to overcome that by finding someone I call an "umbrella person." We'll then cover the sequence of helpers you should engage, and the order in which you should engage them. These helpers include your umbrella person, peer support groups, therapists, specialists, and friends.

OVERCOMING THE OVERWHELM OF ASKING FOR HELP

To understand why asking for help is so hard, let's look at the challenges one faces when signing up for therapy. I first signed up for therapy in early 2018. For the couple of years before that, I knew I had anxiety issues, but I wasn't able to get therapy for them. Why? Because the act of signing up for therapy was too overwhelming. When I considered the terrifying act of digging up my emotions and sharing them with a stranger (albeit a trained one), I realized that doing so would take all of my energy. But then I realized that I also needed to jump through the hoops required to get therapy. I had to pick a therapist, call them, ask for availability, provide my insurance information, fill out a questionnaire, take time off work, and then drive there. Doing all this was about as overwhelming as the idea of doing therapy itself.

I became overwhelmed, trapped between the immense vulnerability required to do therapy and the immense stress of getting myself signed up. Together they were too much for me, so I gave up. I now see that I couldn't have done any better—I was trapped in something I call an "overwhelm checkmate." An overwhelm checkmate is when the vulnerability required to ask for help, combined with the stressful logistics of asking for help, creates a sense of overwhelm too strong to be defeated and prevents you from getting any help at all.

In 2018, I finally got signed up for consistent therapy. How did I manage to do it when I was trapped in an overwhelm checkmate? Well, really, I did it by luck. In late 2017 my new job had an on-campus primary care physician. In early 2018 I went in to meet her for a standard physical. After checking me out, she informed me that while I had no physical health issues, I definitely suffered from mental health challenges like anxiety.

Then she did something that changed my life: she handed me a pamphlet on exactly how to sign up for therapy through my workplace. She let me know that my employer had something called an employee assistance program, and that if I signed up through that, I would get four sessions of therapy for free. Years later, I am immensely grateful for how this chance encounter changed my life.

My interaction with my physician had a specific set of qualities that let me escape my overwhelm checkmate. First, I talked about my need (therapy) with a trusted person in a safe space. Second, that person gave me resources so that signing up for my need was straightforward. This removed one piece of the checkmate because I was no longer overwhelmed by the signing-up process. And with only one piece left—attending therapy—I could muster my energy to sign up for and attend my first therapy session. From there, the rest is history.

YOUR FIRST HELPER: AN UMBRELLA PERSON

I've got a term for what my physician did for me: I call it being an "umbrella person." Imagine you're going to stay at a family member's house for a week, and a friend is driving you and your luggage across town. As you arrive at your destination, rain is pouring down. You would carry an umbrella, but your hands are all full with luggage. So your friend kindly offers to hold an umbrella over the both of you while you carry your luggage inside. After your friend sees that you've safely made it inside, they pull away and go on with their life.

I believe that in order to lug our emotional baggage to places like therapy and support groups, we all need someone to drive us where we're going and hold the umbrella that keeps us dry and safe. Asking for help takes everything you have, and it is terrifying. You need someone there, safely watching over you and making sure you get where you need to go. In my case, my physician "drove" me to my employee assistance program, then kept me safe emotionally by checking to make sure I had signed up.

Before you get specific help with your issues, you need to find an umbrella person who will keep you safe so that you don't get stuck in the overwhelm checkmate.

FINDING YOUR UMBRELLA PERSON

The main qualities of an umbrella person are that they're emotionally intelligent, trustworthy, and care about you. At the end of the day, you just need someone you feel safe around. It's easiest if they're around you a lot. In my previous example, I had already booked the appointment with the physician, so it was easy to talk to her about therapy because she was already there. Nowadays, I have a friend who I have mutual umbrella meetings with every two weeks. I also frequently use Preetha as an umbrella person.

If you're not safe in your personal life with any friends or family, you can use a kind stranger as an umbrella person. The website 7cups.com (https://www.7cups.com/) has over three-hundred thousand trained listeners whom you can talk to anonymously for free. These listeners hold a safe space for you and can help you work through your challenges. If that doesn't appeal to you, you could also follow my posts on social media @woodyrini and make friends with likeminded followers! The great thing about this is that my other followers will probably already know what an umbrella person is. You could even be mutual umbrella buddies with each other like my friend and I are.

You can have as many umbrella people as you want. After all, if you wanted someone to pick you up in the rain, you'd make sure you had multiple friends with cars and umbrellas. If you want to always have someone around to help when you're overwhelmed, develop relationships with multiple umbrella people.

One umbrella person can lead you to another. For example, I needed my physician as my umbrella person to help me sign up for therapy. But after I started seeing my therapist regularly, she became an umbrella person for me too, helping me sign up for a psychiatrist. In this way, I've started with one umbrella person and built a chain of them. You can do the same if you keep following H.E.L.P.

WHAT TO ASK YOUR UMBRELLA PERSON FOR

The goal of having an umbrella person is not to dump all your problems on them. Instead, the goal is to ask them for two things: safety and support. When you're in an overwhelm checkmate, the only way to get out is to feel safe around someone else. By being around someone else who is well regulated and calm, you'll pick up signals of safety and begin to open up. Therefore your first ask of your umbrella person is simply that they listen to you calmly without worrying or trying to fix you.

The second thing you'll ask your umbrella person for is support in engaging an additional help resource. For example, if you're overwhelmed by a career change, you might ask your umbrella person to help you find a career coach in your area. You still sign up for the appointment and pay, but your umbrella person helps point you in the right direction. If you're overwhelmed by mental health issues and need therapy, you'll ask your umbrella person to help you sign up.

If you're nervous about finding your very first umbrella person, don't worry—you already have! It's me! By writing this book for you, I've provided a safe space of sorts where you can start to get help with your overwhelm. I've also provided you with your free H.E.L.P. worksheet and list of mental health resources (both found at http://www.helpimoverwhelmed.com/resources) so that you can be less worried about *how* to get help and instead focus on using your energy to actually get help! You still need to develop at least one solid, real-life umbrella person because I won't be able to personally help every single reader with every problem. But by reading this book and recognizing me as your umbrella person, you're on your way! If you need more umbrella services from me, stay in touch on Instagram @woodyrini.

With safety and support from your umbrella person, you can then move on to the next step, which comes even before going to therapy: joining a peer support group.

THE MAGIC OF PEER SUPPORT GROUPS

I think that peer support groups are one of the most underrated types of help. Peer support groups are free, available both online and in person, offer many social connections in one place, and provide instant relief from overwhelm. You can join at no cost, you can make many friends in a single meeting, and you can feel immediate relief from overwhelm's loneliness by relating to other people with your same challenges.

Before you start asking your umbrella person for help finding therapy, ask them for help finding a peer support group. The reason I believe it's best to start with a peer support group is because you can get started right away, while setting up a therapy appointment can take weeks, if not months. Think of joining a peer support group as training wheels for managing your overwhelm.

WHAT IS A PEER SUPPORT GROUP?

Peer support groups are assemblies of people all facing a similar challenge who meet to talk about it and support one another. Many of these groups meet online via teleconference software, while others meet at local places such as libraries, churches, and schools.

Though support groups tend to vary quite a bit, my research and personal experience have shown that they tend to follow certain patterns that are extremely beneficial in relieving overwhelm.

First, they are based on common struggle, which creates an instant bond between the members. For example, I attend a support group for authors struggling to complete a writing project. Because we all face the same massive challenge, we all feel a deep connection. I've found throughout my life that it is common struggles that bond me with people far more than common hobbies, interests, or successes.

Second, support groups generally give each person a designated time to share while limiting the advice that other people can give to them. Something I hate about everyday life is that it's hard to decide when to talk and when to listen. If I'm talking to someone more talkative than I am, it can be difficult to get a word in edgewise. If I'm talking to someone quiet, I tend to feel like I have to carry the conversation. Either way, I feel on edge because I'm constantly monitoring whether I'm talking too much or too little.

In support groups, everyone gets a chance to share. In a mental health support group that I attend, each member gets four minutes to speak, going in the order that people volunteer. Equally important is that no one is allowed to interrupt the sharer during their time. This makes for an excellent safe space to engage emotions. Imagine having four minutes to say anything you wanted, knowing that you would not be criticized, judged, or interrupted. It's a good feeling, and support groups tend to be excellent at creating this feeling.

Finally, support groups relieve overwhelm because they provide a massive social network of people who get you. Before and after each group meeting I attend, I collect phone numbers of people there. I text them and ask them about their day, and sometimes I even call them. While this seemed scary to me at first, I found it doable because I never had to make small talk. Instead, I chatted about the topic of the support group.

When I'm talking to a friend from my writing group, we discuss writing. When I'm talking to a friend from my mental health group, we go over the steps I'm taking to improve my mental health. Knowing that my conversation partner shares in my common struggle, I'm able to be vulnerable in a way I can't be with close friends or family.

I mentioned in the last chapter that it's easy to isolate when drowning our emotions. Support groups counteract drowning behaviors because they're built around deep social connections. They're also great practice for making friends in the real world. I've found that I have more confidence talking to neighbors and local friends because I've practiced being vulnerable in the safe space of my support group.

There's a certain magic about peer support groups. You enter alone, and you leave with a family who gets you. You leave with connections to people who have the exact same challenge as you do, who are overwhelmed by the exact same things. Simply knowing you're not alone counteracts the Ultimate Overwhelming Thought of "I should be able to do this, but I can't" and replaces it with the Ultimate Empowering Thought of "I can do this, but I need help." If you find the right support group, I bet you'll feel a profound relief from your overwhelm after a single meeting. I call that magic.

ARE THERE REALLY PEER SUPPORT GROUPS THAT WORK FOR ME? WHERE DO I FIND THEM?

You may wonder at this point if your specific overwhelming challenge has a support group. Don't worry—whatever is overwhelming you is very likely to have an online support group that you can join. As I mentioned earlier, I even found a support group with people who were struggling to finish a book!

Finding the right support group is as easy as Googling "peer support group for _____." Just insert whatever your overwhelm current is in the blank. When I wanted to find a writers' group, I searched "peer support group for writers" and found a meeting where writers helped each other and talked about their challenges. Because of the COVID-19 pandemic, almost all support groups have an online option now, which means no matter where you live you can get access.

In an effort to be the best umbrella person I can for you, I've made a quick list of example peer support groups for you to review. Remember, this is a small sample of what's out there!

Some examples of peer support groups are:

- For mental health issues, the Mental Health America Affiliate Center: https://arc.mhanational.org/find-an-affiliate
- Also for mental health issues, the National Alliance on Mental Illness (NAMI): https://www.nami.org/Support-Education/Mental-Health-Education/NAMI-Peer-to-Peer
- For mental health issues and addiction, the SAMHSA (Substance Abuse and Mental Health Services Administration) helpline: https://www.samhsa.gov/find-help/national-helpline
- Twelve-step groups modeled after Alcoholics Anonymous: (https://en.wikipedia.org/wiki/List_of_twelve-step_groups)
- For parenting: https://www.parentshelpingparents.org/virtual-support-groups
- As a catch-all, Meetup.com:
  o https://www.meetup.com/
  o For career transitions: https://www.meetup.com/topics/career-transition/
  o Meetup is also useful for finding identity-based support groups, such as racial/gender/sexual identity peer support and activities groups

HELPING LOVED ONES GET SUPPORT

I know that some of you may be reading this book to better understand how to help someone else, and I'd like to let you know that support groups tend to offer options for friends and family of those with an overwhelming challenge as well. For example, the National Alliance on Mental Illness offers a peer support group for those with a loved one with mental health challenges. (https://www.nami.org/Support-Education/Support-Groups/NAMI-Family-Support-Group) Or, if you're concerned that someone in your life is having a problem with alcohol and you'd like to help them, you could find support at Al-Anon. (https://al-anon.org/newcomers/how-can-i-help-my/)

These family resources are available for almost every peer support group that exists. Remember, these support groups are not geared toward helping you control or manipulate the other people in your life. Instead, they're geared toward helping you deal with *your* overwhelm that results from your loved one's challenge. Even if you're reading this book primarily to help a loved one, you'll get the best results if you keep working your H.E.L.P. method on *yourself* by signing up for a family support group and therapy for you!

BUILDING YOUR THERAPY NETWORK

After you've found an umbrella person and a peer support group, the next step toward escaping your overwhelm current is finding professional help.

The most robust mental health plan includes a therapist, a psychiatrist, and a specialized trauma therapist. Think that sounds like too much? Think of it this way: for your physical health, you have a primary care physician and a dentist. You probably also see some kind of specialist (cardiologist, gastroenterologist, OBGYN, etc.) for issues specific to your medical needs. If you see at least three professionals regularly for your physical health, why should you not do the same for your mental health?

In this section I'll outline why having those three team members (therapist, psychiatrist, and trauma specialist) will bring you enormous relief from overwhelm and increase your quality of life. But don't worry about finding these team members instantly; it may take you months to find a good therapist and psychiatrist, and years before you're ready for trauma therapy. That's ok! Engage these resources on a timeline that makes sense for you.

WHAT TO EXPECT WHEN SIGNING UP FOR THERAPY

Having a therapist is like having a general practitioner for your mental health. To me, they're equally important. Every person should have a GP to keep their body healthy and a therapist to keep their mind healthy. Obviously, this is not necessarily easy to do in current society, but that's because overwhelm currents and trauma are far less understood than physical health problems. Another way to think about it is to remember that your therapist is your lifeguard: they have the perspective to see your overwhelm current, the training to make a diagnosis, and the specialized tools to treat you.

Here's what you can expect to happen when you sign up for therapy. First, you'll need to call your umbrella person and let them know you need help. Signing up for therapy takes some work, just like signing up for a new primary care physician does. You'll start by picking a therapist, finding their availability, and then booking an appointment.

After that, you'll likely receive some kind of questionnaire about your mental health. Answer honestly and return it to the therapist's office or bring it with you to your appointment, whatever they tell you to do. Throughout this initial process, be sure to lean on your umbrella person for support.

Things you can ask your umbrella person to do when signing up for therapy:

- find a nearby therapist's office accepting patients with your insurance
- research the cost of your therapist
- listen nonjudgmentally while you talk through your fears of going to therapy
- keep you honest when you're tempted to skip an appointment or give up
- help you with kids, work, housework, food, or anything that would make your life easier so that you can dedicate energy to getting therapy

If you're busy at work and have to make time for your appointment, be sure to find an umbrella person you trust at work too. Ask them to cover for you while you're gone, and let them know you'll do the same for them when they have important appointments. Remember, there's no shame in asking for help—it's necessary!

When you go to your first therapy appointment, you'll sit in a quiet room with the therapist and go through an initial intake survey. They'll likely ask you all kinds of questions about your personal life. Remember, this person is trained to keep your confidentiality and treat you with the utmost respect. You are safe sharing with them. It may feel like you're giving your internal secrets to a stranger, but you'll get comfortable with it. After all, it feels strange getting blood drawn by a doctor, but we're willing to do it because we know they'll provide a diagnosis. The same is true of a therapist.

Most of your first appointment will be taken up by the intake session. That's why I recommend that at minimum you try two therapy appointments before questioning whether it's a good fit for you. Over the course of my life I've seen many therapists, and each time the first visit felt unsettling, but from the second on I felt much better.

After the second appointment, decide whether you feel the therapist is the right person to be helping you. At the first therapy office I went to, I saw three different therapists and only felt comfortable with one of them. Having a therapist is a relationship, and if it's not working for you, better to break it off and try someone else than keep going.

How a Therapist Helps You

As you continue with your therapist, you'll gain a few key benefits. First, you'll receive an actual diagnosis of any mental disorder you have. When I visited my therapist, she diagnosed me with generalized anxiety disorder. Once you have a diagnosis, you can learn how to get help for it. Our society portrays mental health diagnoses as being liabilities, taboo, or shameful, but when you think about it, that doesn't make any sense. Is it shameful to be diagnosed with asthma or a vitamin deficiency by your GP? No, instead it's a relief— you know what's wrong and so can get help in the form of an inhaler or vitamin supplements. The doctor helps you by diagnosing the issue and giving you something to help it. This is exactly what your therapist will do.

I've always found that having a formal diagnosis for my mental health conditions has given me relief by helping me realize I'm not alone. Other people had to have had the same challenge as me, or the diagnosis wouldn't exist. Getting a diagnosis also helped me dispel some of the frantic, panicked confusion that always came with being overwhelmed. I no longer had to feel confused when I thought about all the emotions and worries I was experiencing. Instead, I could say, "I have generalized anxiety disorder, and I'm getting therapy for it!" Being able to say this was empowering because it gave a name to my experience, which then became much more manageable than something scarily unknown. Diagnosing my disorder—naming my overwhelm—brought immense relief.

Once you have a diagnosis, you'll then receive therapy to help you with your disorder. Notice that I didn't say "cure" your disorder. Not every medical or mental health issue is curable. Consider the person with asthma; they don't get cured of asthma, but they do receive an inhaler and medication to help prevent the asthma from interfering with their life. It's the same with mental health. You receive therapy so that you have the tools to deal with your mental health challenges, not so that you can be perfectly cured.

One way therapists provide immense relief from overwhelm is by giving you a dedicated hour of completely safe space. Even if you simply talk about your day to your therapist, you'll feel relieved afterwards. Talking to your therapist may be the first conversation in your entire life where you can say exactly what you feel without worrying about retaliation, as therapists are paid to listen to whatever you say without judgment. Talking freely will give you the time to bring up your emotions and start engaging them. You can dispel the extreme emotions and start to develop more regulated, helpful ones. Also, if you're in your therapist's office, you're not on your own panicking or falling into drowning behaviors. Just by showing up for an hour you halt the panic, engage emotions, and receive help. That's all three of the steps so far rolled up into one!

The second thing a therapist does is use specific therapeutic techniques to address your mental health issues. For example, if you struggle with social gatherings, your therapist might use cognitive behavioral therapy to help you acclimate. This would include asking you to jot down your fearful thoughts about the social gathering, then analyzing how such thoughts aren't true by pointing out the cognitive distortions you have. For example, you may believe that everyone at the social gathering is judging your outfit, but your therapist can help you see that you're self-magnifying; other people don't really mind what you wear.

Escaping overwhelm requires constant dedication to chipping away at the distorted thoughts that we develop while overwhelmed. Therapists have the tools and training to help us chip away at these distorted thoughts (which are often similar to the Ultimate Overwhelming Thought), and to help us start thinking more in terms of the Ultimate Empowering Thought. Our therapist is like the lifeguard throwing us a flotation device—but we must grab it by accepting and using the techniques our therapist gives us.

A comprehensive list of therapeutic techniques is beyond the scope of this book, but there are many great resources available online if you want to learn more about how therapy works.

THE BENEFITS OF CONSIDERING MENTAL HEALTH MEDICATION

After you get in a rhythm with your therapist, you'll probably want to make an appointment with either a psychiatrist or a primary care physician to be evaluated for mental health medication. Like therapy, mental health medication carries an unnecessary stigma because mental health disorders are falsely portrayed as less real than other disorders. You might be surprised to find that according to the CDC, around 15.8 percent of adults in the US took mental health medication in 2019. Medication is popular and helps many people.

As with any medication, you should only take mental health medication based on conversations with a licensed doctor. This means either a psychiatrist or a primary care physician. Therapists cannot prescribe medication for you unless they are also a doctor. A psychiatrist is a doctor who specializes in mental health medication. They will evaluate you in a similar manner to a therapist and then decide whether to recommend a specific mental health medication for you. If getting a psychiatrist appointment seems unrealistic for you, your primary care physician can give you a prescription too. They might not know as many details about the medication, but they will work with you to keep you safe. Only take medication when you've received a valid prescription; if you don't have the education that a doctor does, self-medicating can too easily become both a drowning behavior and dangerous.

You may still be skeptical about medication, but don't worry, I used to be a skeptic too! I didn't pop out of the womb waving a foam finger that said, "Go Team Medication!" I was doubtful of medication even after I started therapy. At my second visit with my therapist in 2018, she recommended medication. I politely told her that I wanted to "beat this anxiety on my own." I felt like it was cheating to take a pill to solve my mental health issues. This was probably due to my internalized desire to be perfect, on the first try, by myself (the Ultimate Overwhelming Thought). In reality, my attempt to "beat this anxiety on my own" manifested in criticizing myself for being anxious (a panic behavior) and playing video games to avoid my own thoughts and emotions (a drowning behavior).

At my next appointment, my therapist brought up medication again. She said, "Woody, I care about you, and if you don't at least consider medication, I don't think you'll get the results you want from therapy." Well, as skeptical as I was, I chose to trust her. I signed up for a psychiatrist appointment, and after being evaluated, I was prescribed a standard mental health drug.

Everyone's medication journey is different, but mine started with a bang. Almost from the moment I started, I felt transformed. It was as if the frenetic, crazy, panicked thinking slowed down. I had previously been consistently overwhelmed by conversations that replayed in my head dozens of times. After starting medication, these conversations nearly ceased.

I cannot emphasize enough the enormous amount of relief I felt after taking medication. I had been worried taking a pill was cheating. Well, after taking it, I felt so good that I didn't care if I was cheating—I was going to do it anyway! That relief from overwhelm that I talked about as my number-one desire? I felt it from medication in an immediately tangible way.

After learning more about how medication works, I realized that not only was it not cheating, it wasn't going to irreversibly change who I was. Instead, medication helped lift me out of the overwhelmed state I was in, allowing me to engage my emotions and get more out of therapy. Medication added peace and meaning to my life!

In this scenario, mental health solutions once again parallel physical health ones. Taking medication for your mental health is like taking medication for a physical problem. If you take a statin to lower your cholesterol, you still need to work on your diet and exercise. If you take an anti-inflammatory drug for a torn ACL post-surgery, you still need to do your rehab exercises. Medication alone is not enough, but therapy without medication may not have the strongest effects. Just as healing a physical issue sometimes requires pills and therapy, so does healing a mental health issue!

For more information on the details of how mental health medications work, check out this link from Mental Health America: https://www.mhanational.org/medication.

EMDR AND BRAINSPOTTING™ THERAPY: NEW THERAPY METHODS THAT WORK WONDERS

The final member of my personal therapy trio is a trauma therapist who uses eye movement techniques. While most people have some idea of how talk therapy works, and some understanding of medication, many don't know about trauma therapies like EMDR (Eye Movement Desensitization and Reprocessing) or Brainspotting™. I didn't try these therapies until recently, but my life has already been changed so much by them that I can't help but shout their praises from the mountaintops.

Before I dive into the techniques and what they've done for me, I'd like to let you know how I define trauma. I think of trauma as overwhelm from the past that has concentrated into such a dense clump of current overwhelm that it requires specific care to resolve. After all, even if I work hard to be less overwhelmed now, what about the first twenty-nine years of my life? Surely I was overwhelmed some during those years, often badly! I believe that all of us have some leftover overwhelm, which is generally referred to as trauma. Trauma therapy is a specific type of therapy that addresses these clumps of overwhelm that are stuck in us.

EMDR and Brainspotting™ therapies are unique in that they focus not just on talking but on stimulating deeper sections of the brain using eye movements. In EMDR, patients follow a light or pointer back and forth across their field of vision as they attempt to reprocess a traumatic memory. In Brainspotting™, the therapist moves a pointer around the patient's field of vision until they find a "spot" where the patient's trauma or emotions seem to be activated.

Look, I know it sounds bizarre, but this stuff works. EMDR is new, having been invented in 1987, but it's already been scientifically validated by researchers in many different independent studies, which can be found online. Using eye movements to stimulate areas of the brain does indeed help patients reprocess trauma.

My therapist also uses the technique of Brainspotting™ (https://Brainspotting.com/). She holds a retractable pointer (like a teacher might use to point at a whiteboard) with a green ball on the end, and she moves it around my field of vision. She asks me to focus on a specific feeling in my body that I want to process, and when the feeling is the strongest, I tell her to stop the pointer. I then sit still, without talking, as I process my feelings and notice what's happening in my body. After a few minutes, I start to tell her what I notice in my body. I also tell her what thoughts come up. Amazingly, within about twenty minutes of looking at the pointer and engaging my emotions, I feel my body relax. It's as if the trauma has been processed and I'm breaking down those clumps of overwhelm.

Notice that my experience with trauma therapy is a tangible, physical feeling. I'd consider it similar to getting a deep tissue massage. The massage therapist presses on your body's trigger points, and while it hurts in the moment, you feel a release and a relaxation after the massage is over. Brainspotting™ seems to be much the same to me. In Brainspotting™, I find a spot where my body is activated, I hold on to that spot, and the spot slowly releases!

You may wonder whether you have any spots of trauma, or whether you can skip this. My belief is that if you have emotional drowning behaviors, that means you have trauma, which means you need trauma therapy. If you're feeling skeptical, revisit your H.E.L.P. worksheet and consider all your drowning behaviors. Consider your alcohol use, your screen time, your workaholism, or whatever you use to drown. I think you're doing these activities not just to escape from overwhelm in the present but to escape from trauma from the past.

You can feel relaxed, free, and amazing without any emotional drowning whatsoever. I definitely feel like I'm on my way to this, but I still go to trauma therapy regularly because I still feel it working. I can't recommend it highly enough. I genuinely believe that because life is so overwhelming, every single one of us ends up with stored trauma, and trauma therapy is the best way to work through that.

FINDING THERAPY THAT MATCHES YOUR BUDGET: SECRET WAYS TO REDUCE THERAPY COSTS

While I've made the argument that therapy is as important as physical care, that doesn't change the fact that you may not be able to pay for both. You have to pay your doctor and your dentist and whatever specialists you use, and just dealing with that can be a hassle. How will you find the money to also pay for therapy? This is a valid question and deserves a good answer. After all, standard therapy rates are around $150 an hour! That's far more than anyone would like to pay out of pocket.

LEVERAGING YOUR EMPLOYER FOR AFFORDABLE THERAPY

The easiest way to get affordable therapy is through your employer. If you have a fairly good insurance plan, therapy might be covered just like a doctor visit. You may only have to pay thirty-five to fifty dollars per appointment, which is an excellent deal considering the benefits you'll receive from therapy. Remember, your umbrella person should be able to help you deal with the effort required to sign up, including figuring out how much you would have to pay to be seen.

Another option is something employers often have called an employee assistance program. This is where employers offer employees free, special benefits, often based on helping them with life and mental health issues. I got my first four therapy sessions for free via an employee assistance program, and this was definitely a factor in my decision to start therapy. It took one more worry off the table. If you're curious about this, check out your company website or contact your HR representative.

If you're a student, then it's very likely that you can get therapy for free or at a low cost through your university. When I had my depressive episode as a college student, I was referred by campus health services to one of the two on-campus therapists who were available to me free of charge. Even if you're a part-time student, be sure to check what kind of therapy options your university offers. Students get perks in many areas of life, and therapy is certainly not an exception.

These are the three easiest ways to get affordable therapy: through a good insurance plan, through an employee assistance plan, and through university services. But what if you have a high deductible insurance plan, or one that doesn't cover mental health, and there's no institutional access? Don't worry—we can find a solution for you. We'll just have to get a little creative!

MORE CREATIVE WAYS TO GET THERAPY COSTS COVERED

If you can't get affordable therapy from the ways listed above, the first thing you should do is evaluate whether you belong to any type of special group that gets supported by nonprofits. For example, let's say you're a firefighter and you make a small salary and have a high deductible on your medical insurance. Guess what—you're a first responder! That means you qualify to get completely free therapy through the nonprofit 911 At Ease International. You can pop over to their website and sign up. (https://911aei.org/)

How did I figure that out? Easy. I used the website for the National Alliance on Mental Illness, a group that collects resources to help people with mental health challenges. I used the directory in the "My Journey" page at the NAMI website. (https://nami.org/Your-Journey) I navigated to frontline workers and then to first responders, and there it was. The first thing you should do when seeking mental health resources on a budget is comb through that "My Journey" page and note all the resources available to you.

But let's say you're not a firefighter or any other job that gets covered by a nonprofit. You're just an ordinary person who needs help with mental health. You and your umbrella person will need to take matters into your own hands by asking therapy practices and universities whether there are any affordable options available.

Did you know that many practicing therapists save at least one slot for clients in financial need, and that they offer these clients free or reduced-cost therapy services?

It's true. Therapists are kind people who want to help, so they make space for those who need a little financial assistance. Therapy offices don't necessarily advertise these slots, though, so you'll have to call the office and ask, "Do you have any therapists offering sliding-scale or reduced-cost therapy for someone in financial need?" If you ask enough local offices, I'm willing to bet you can find a therapist who will take you on at a fraction of the full price.

One more option is to call local universities and ask if they have any therapy interns giving therapy at a reduced cost. Students getting their degree in counseling must complete a certain number of intern hours, and while they aren't full therapists yet, they'll likely be able to help you quite a bit. You can often work with these students at rates as low as twenty dollars an hour.

Oh, and there's one final option that you might try if nothing else works. If you have any family members in a better financial situation than you are, you might ask if they'll cover some of your therapy expenses.

If your issue is not money but time, consider an online therapy option. Just like support groups are online now, so are therapists. There are sites full of online therapists such as betterhelp.com. If you Google "online therapy," ads for online therapy will come right to the top of your screen. These online sites often have more flexible scheduling than traditional offices.

Remember, when you're seeking therapy, *lean on your umbrella person*. Have someone in your corner exploring these options for you. Find a friend who will call ten therapy offices for reduced rates and free options. I believe that with enough perseverance, you can find therapy at an affordable rate.

Also note that as you panic and drown emotionally less, you'll save time and money that you can use to find therapy. When I chose to stop drowning my emotions through excessive video games, I was able to save over a hundred dollars a month. I also got back many hours per week that I could use to schedule and go to the appointments.

Don't give up if it seems like there's absolutely no time or money for therapy in your schedule—ask yourself how you can use your umbrella person, along with quitting panic and drowning behaviors, to make it work.

ROUNDING OUT YOUR HELP SQUAD WITH SPECIALISTS AND FRIENDS

At this point, you understand how to get your core help. You will get an umbrella person, a support group, and a therapist. These core resources will change your life in ways you never thought possible. Once you're rolling with your core resources, all you need to do is keep asking for help in all the different ways you need it.

Some examples of additional specialists I have reached out to when overwhelmed are:

- career and life coaches
- nutritionist and dietician
- massage therapist
- chiropractor
- dog trainer

Of course, not everyone has the time and money to book specialists. Instead, it's perfectly fine to be creative and get help at low-to-no cost. Some ways I do this are:

- mutual life coaching with a friend who also loves business
- a colleague who serves as my business mentor
- getting cooking lessons and recipes from a family member

As you feel more and more comfortable thanks to your new help resources, you'll probably be more interested in cultivating social relationships. I know that when I was totally overwhelmed, I didn't make time for friends. I let relationships drop and isolated myself to play video games. Now that I have help, I make sure to explore my world. I schedule dates with my wife and spend time on the phone with friends and family.

Just having regular conversations with people you care about is a way of getting help. Remember, the goal of this whole H.E.L.P. process is to relieve us of our overwhelm so that we can enjoy life. We want to live in a state of relief, realizing our potential. Spending time talking to friends and family helps us engage that target state and strengthen it!

At this point, fill out the portion of the H.E.L.P. worksheet shown below.

I, _____ , accept that I need help. I am willing to ask for help.

The person I would like to ask to be my umbrella person is:

_____

I will ask them via _____ (text, phone, in person), at this time: _____

The peer group I would like to join is:

_____

The first meeting I will attend is on _____ (day) at _____ (time), and is located at _____ (physical or online meeting location).

I am willing and open to receive professional help.

The type of professional help I need is: _____.

I will ask my umbrella person _____ to help me engage them by doing this: _____

CHAPTER SEVEN

P IS FOR PATIENTLY FLOAT AND PARALLEL SWIM

E ven if you diligently ask for help and are completely willing to let others help you out of your overwhelm current, you still face the same problem that the swimmer in the rip current faces—you need to survive until help gets there! In the last chapter, you've done the equivalent of yelling for a lifeguard. But you still need to understand how to tread water, or perhaps swim slightly away from the rip current, so that you can still be afloat when the lifeguard arrives.

In this chapter we'll cover the two main types of behaviors we can do on our own while we wait for our help to come. These are self-calming behaviors, which are the equivalent of patiently floating, and self-improvement behaviors, which are the equivalent of swimming parallel to the shore (i.e. perpendicular to the rip current). In this section, I'll tell a lot of personal stories about how I discovered my different floating and swimming behaviors. Each behavior I list is also something that may work for you, so I'd encourage you to give it a try. However, every person is different. What soothes me may make you anxious. What feels productive to me may feel pointless to you. After reading through this chapter, you'll be asked to come up with patiently floating and parallel swim behaviors that work for you; get creative and come up with ideas of your own.

LEARNING TO FLOAT

At its core, a patiently floating behavior is anything you do to healthily reduce your overwhelm or protect yourself during an overwhelming situation. A simple example would be handling a social anxiety panic attack by walking away and getting a breather. I know that when I struggled with panic at social events, I used to force myself to stay and talk despite feeling totally frozen inside. I thought that forcing myself to endure the event—to confront my overwhelm head on—was the way to get better. Now I realize that I needed help, and that in the moment, the best thing I could have done would have been to take space outside to breathe and unfreeze.

Float behaviors are the healthy version of emotional drowning behaviors. Both try to reduce overwhelm in the moment. But while drowning behaviors avoid emotions and make overwhelm increase in the long run, floating behaviors engage emotions and make overwhelm decrease in the long run. When you're floating, you should be feeling your feelings!

CALMING MENTAL ACTIVITIES FOR YOUR ROUTINE

While taking a beat to calm down is always a useful floating behavior, it's even better if we make floating techniques part of our daily routine so that we are calmer in general. One of the first ways I did this when I was overwhelmed at work was by making guided meditation a part of my workday routine. I worked at a computer and could take fifteen-minute breaks when necessary. Instead of scrolling the news on my breaks (a drowning behavior), I spent them on a guided meditation with the Headspace app (a floating behavior). Meditation is scary to me, and I personally never have the willpower needed to silently meditate when I'm overwhelmed. That's why I prefer apps to guide me through my meditation; it's a form of asking for help because I'm walked through the meditative steps I need to take. And doing it regularly made it easier to draw on those meditative practices when I was in an overwhelming situation. Try Headspace, Calm, or any app that works for you.

Another way to remain calm is to make soothing music a bigger part of your daily routine. My music game stepped up in 2020 when I subscribed to Spotify. The reason I love using a music-streaming service is that they have curated playlists. If I want to listen to relaxing music from the early 2000s, there's already a playlist for that. If I want to listen to today's hits, there's a playlist for that too. If I'm working on something that requires no distractions, I listen to classical music. I recommend you make your music life easier by finding a streaming service and exploring curated playlists. Many services like Spotify, Pandora, and YouTube Music offer free plans, so spending money isn't necessary unless you want to remove ads or access advanced features. A free service can work perfectly well to calm you down.

SOOTHING PHYSICAL ACTIVITIES FOR YOUR ROUTINE

Another underestimated way to survive overwhelm is to routinely practice physically soothing activities. After all, the overwhelmed state we're trying to avoid isn't just a state of mind—it's a full-body response. As I've grown in my floating practices, I've started to see that finding ways to soothe my body, no matter how silly I look, reduces my overwhelm until my next support meeting or therapy appointment.

The most surprising and simple soothing method I've discovered is rocking. I'll sit in a recliner or rocking chair and rock the chair up and down with my legs. When I'm Brainspotting™, I rock myself side to side by swiveling in my office chair. When I first started these practices, I felt like an idiot. Who sits and rocks himself like a baby? But like many of the practices in this book, rocking felt so good that it became a regular part of my routine. I feel that rocking makes me feel safe and held, like a baby. It also makes me relaxed and calm. Now I schedule time each day where I listen to soothing music and rock myself in a recliner.

Another easy and incredibly effective way I soothe myself is by taking baths. I run the hot water and add three extra ingredients: a bath bomb, some bubble bath, and Epsom salt. A bath bomb is a tennis ball–sized block of salts and oils that dissolves in your tub, usually with a pretty color and fragrance. Bubble bath is a little more obvious; I like to add lavender-scented bubble bath. Finally, Epsom salt is a form of magnesium that dissolves in water and eases your aches and pains. The combination of these three enhancements makes a bath a luxurious experience!

Buying all that stuff, making the bath, and taking it might sound like a lot of time and effort, but that's exactly why I find taking baths effective. Once in the bath, I feel physically forced to relax. Relaxing is no longer up to my mind—it's happening to my body whether I like it or not! Taking a bath is also a further example of a behavior which I never would do if I didn't know help was coming. When I take a bath now, I know that even if I tried to use that time for something productive, I would just end up doing a panic or drowning behavior. By taking a bath, I put myself in a situation where I'm not only forced to relax, I'm not able to screw things up by panicking.

Of course, any soothing or calming activity counts as a patiently floating activity. Go to the spa. Get a fancy haircut at a nice salon. Get a manicure or pedicure. Go on a walk or run. Have a picnic in nature. Choose the soothing activities that work for you! Counteract the overwhelm not by drowning your emotions but by sitting with them in the most soothing safe space you can find.

Sitting with your emotions really is as simple as feeling them without fighting them off or logically analyzing them. I'll sit with my emotions by taking a bath and feeling tension in my chest from being afraid, or love in my heart from feeling relaxed, or excitement in my brain and limbs from feeling eager to take on the day's activities. When my feelings become too much for me, I start to think about how I'm going to tell my support group or my therapist about them, and this always helps me feel less overwhelmed. This is why getting H.E.L.P. is so crucial, and why self-soothing can only take you so far!

If you're confused about the difference between soothing activities and activities that drown your emotions in excessive pleasure, just ask yourself: is this activity a form of self-care that makes me feel nourished and loved? I find that when I'm drowning my emotions, I know instinctively that what I'm doing is not taking care of myself. And I find that when I'm soothing, even though I'm scared of all the emotions I'm feeling, my body feels loved and cared for. Always look for the self-care feeling when doing a soothing activity!

PARALLEL SWIM: HOW TO USE SELF-IMPROVEMENT ACTIVITIES TO MAKE GETTING HELP A LITTLE EASIER

Now that you have a repertoire of calming and soothing float activities, it's time to move on to the parallel swim portion of this step in H.E.L.P. Doing these activities is critical because I often find myself having extra energy and the need to do something that seems productive while waiting for help. I no longer want to do panic behaviors, so when I have that productivity itch in my brain, I have to scratch it. These are the activities I use to scratch that itch while also moving myself farther away from my overwhelm so that my help can be more effective once it gets to me.

Parallel swimming adds a lot of meaning to my life, and I can often find this meaning even in the midst of my overwhelm current.

PERSONALITY TESTS

The first-ever parallel swim activity I used was taking personality tests. I remember sitting in my office feeling overwhelmed by the stagnancy of my career, but also feeling too agitated to meditate or do something soothing. I had extra energy, and I needed to do something with my brain! Normally I would have used video games or news to drown myself, or I would have kept working on emails or assignments that were already good enough. One day, I had a passing thought: what if I took a personality test?

I searched online and found the Myers Briggs Type Inventory (MBTI) on 16personalities.com. As you might guess from the name of the website, the MBTI sorts you into one of sixteen personality types based on four different attributes. After I took a brief questionnaire about my lifestyle and interests, the website told me that I was an INFJ personality type. It then presented me with pages of information on what that meant: what I liked (helping people), what I didn't like (menial tasks), what I was good at (public speaking and counseling), what I was not good at (corporate computer programming jobs—oops!). I had so much fun reading this personality profile; it was like someone finally got me.

I didn't feel like the test results were forcing me to be someone or putting me in a box. Rather, I felt like by getting my test results, I was placed into a peer group of people who understood my whole self. While I didn't have a face-to-face peer support group, I could picture all the other INFJs out there dealing with the same struggles I was, having the same hopes and dreams that I had. This was liberating and energizing.

Obviously, knowing my personality type was not going to convince my boss that I deserved a promotion or revitalize my career at my company. But it was the equivalent of swimming parallel—I felt productive and useful, and I gained insights that I could use at whatever my next job was. This is the goal of parallel swim activities!

I always recommend personality tests to clients because I think it's one of the quickest ways for them to feel understood, which helps them feel less overwhelmed. I recommend you give them a try too.

PODCASTS AND SELF-IMPROVEMENT BOOKS

Podcasts and self-improvement books offer similar stimulation as a personality test but in a different flavor. The best thing about podcasts is that you can listen to them when traveling or doing menial chores. Of course, you can do the same with an audiobook. Just pop in your earbuds while you're doing laundry, commuting, or exercising.

There's a specific technique I use when reading/listening to self-improvement content that I call the "spiderweb technique." Whenever I listen to a podcast, I'll pick its one or two most interesting ideas and explore them more. I may listen to an hour-long podcast and enjoy the whole experience, but then I'll home in on a book or resource that was recommended and search that up. From that book, I may find a business class or another podcast. By staying curious, I constantly find new ideas that stimulate my brain. I call this "building my spiderweb" because each discovery, each new resource, connects to the others in a big network. Consciously building my web lets me see how my self-improvement techniques all relate to one another. You can do this too!

PROFESSIONAL SKILLS

The third thing you can do to parallel swim out of your overwhelm current is to learn professional skills. This might include computer programming, graphic design, customer service, entrepreneurship, technical writing, or skills applicable to your career. Basically, if you feel overwhelmed and like you're stagnating in life, learn the skills you want to apply at a new job. If you're a stay-at-home parent with a house full of crazy kids who yearns to get back to work, learn skills you think could be useful if you did enter the workforce!

When I was stagnating at work in 2017, I started signing up for every single career development class that my workplace offered. I took classes on how to give good presentations and speak publicly. I took classes on Microsoft Excel. I used an online subscription my workplace offered to take a course on how to blog professionally, using that information to write guest blog posts for self-help websites. In one business class, I wrote a sheet of notes that became the genesis of this book! By stimulating my mind in as many ways as I could, I developed skills that were useful for the future even though I was totally stuck and overwhelmed in the present. If you keep learning valuable skills, you'll find a way to put them to use.

HOUSE AND HOME SKILLS

The last main category of parallel swim activities I use is house and home skills. I'm constantly developing my ability to take better care of my home, manage my personal finances, and take care of my family. As part of my journey toward escaping my overwhelm, I had to quit my day job because it was causing too much overwhelm. I thought my business skills would lead me to immediate riches, but this wasn't the case. I struggled financially and relied on Preetha for financial support. I was in a huge overwhelm current in my career, and I knew it would take time to get out. What did I do? I worked my butt off at developing house and home skills.

My house and home skills are the crucial parallel swim activity that gives me the breathing room needed to write this book. I do dishes like a machine. I take care of the dog's vet care and training. I organize our personal finances in a budget planner called Mint so that we always know, down to the last penny, where we spend our money. I also set up automatic payments for our credit cards and automatic transfers to our retirement and investments accounts. I make Preetha dinner and baths. I always fill up her water bottle whenever she needs it. I put gas in her car. In essence, I am a talented home manager and an extremely supportive husband.

I say all that to show you that you can get creative with parallel swim activities. I never imagined that I would be a home manager. But faced with complete overwhelm at work, I knew that I had to reset and start over, and that I had to wait for a lot of help before I got where I wanted to go. Almost three years after quitting my job, I'm publishing my book and starting to make my own way financially. (And I'm using all of those professional skills I learned even when I was stagnant in my career, such as writing and internet marketing.) But I was able to navigate what life offered me by seeing that my big opportunity to stay out of the rip was building my home management skills.

If you choose the appropriate parallel swim activities, they will build your confidence and momentum so that when you finally get helped out of your current, you can hit the ground running, just like I have with this book. Start thinking about what actions feel like swimming parallel for you!

WHEN YOU STILL CAN'T STAY AFLOAT, YOU NEED TO CUT THE WEIGHT!

The truth is that facing overwhelming challenges is really, really hard. It's much easier to drown your emotions with the television than it is to engage your emotions, stop panicking, and ask for help. Even after you do everything in this book, you'll still have periods where you feel you just can't keep going, and where you turn back to your emotional drowning behaviors. The next time you find yourself coming out of a three-hour-long social media scrolling session, or a week of drinking every night to forget your troubles, or a compulsive workaholic frenzy, you need to reread this section.

When nothing else is working to keep you afloat, you need to cut out whatever is weighing you down so that you become more buoyant. This means examining every single thing in your life and cutting out whatever is the heaviest optional weight, which I consider the thing that causes you the most overwhelm but will not directly harm anyone else if you stop doing it.

In my case, the first thing I had to cut was social activities. I used to go out to dinner parties at least once a week. These dinner parties had wonderful people and conversation, but because I was so anxious in social situations, they made me a nervous wreck. I was totally overwhelmed by just the idea of going to them. Almost inevitably, after these gatherings I would pick a fight with Preetha. We would have a miserable night and the next few days I would spend in a trance playing video games or watching TV. No matter how much I tried to reengage my emotions and float, I just couldn't do it. I was overwhelmed.

So I told Preetha I wasn't going to go to the dinner parties anymore. She was upset. She told me that she wanted to go, and that she would look bad if she showed up without me. After all, most of the people at the dinner parties were couples. But though it displeased her, I stuck to my guns and stopped attending these events. It hurt, but I knew that if I drowned, I was no good to her anyway. The result in the long run was worth her immediate displeasure. And at the end of the day, it was only a dinner party—I wasn't actively harming my wife by choosing not to go.

As I continued to seek help and work on my own trauma, I realized that I was also letting people in my life overwhelm me on a regular basis. Even people I loved and respected sometimes acted as weights, making me feel overwhelmed when talking with or being around them. Over the past year, I've made a dedicated effort to set clear and strict boundaries on the time I spend with people who make me feel overwhelmed, family included. I recommend that you do this as well.

Note that you're not blaming friends or family for your overwhelm. Rather, you're taking space for yourself. You're also not abandoning them. If the people making you feel weighed down are functioning adults, then they're responsible for their own life just like you are. Your guilt for "abandoning" them is probably a people-pleasing panic behavior, rooted in trauma that you need to explore in therapy. The encouraging news is that the more you work on the H.E.L.P. process, the more energy you'll have, and the better you'll be able to interact with these people! You aren't deserting them forever; you'll return when you're ready.

As part of cutting weight during my most overwhelmed moments, I also decided to take a break from social media. I stopped posting, stopped scrolling, and stopped reading. I even quit visiting news websites. For me, reading social media and news felt like an obligation so that I could keep up with others and talk about socially relevant topics. But in order to make my world as simple and low-stress as possible, I had to quit social media for over a year just to manage my overwhelm!

In the most extreme example of cutting weight, I quit my job in 2019 because I knew I was drowning. If Preetha was slightly miffed when I ditched social interactions, she was terrified when I told her I wanted to quit my job. I didn't quit on a whim. I first brought up the idea in a financial-planning conversation with her in the fall of 2018, over a year before I quit. Never make life-altering decisions in the heat of a moment. Take months, a year, or more to plan your big moves. I thought deeply about quitting my job because I knew that unlike quitting dinner parties, leaving my job could actively harm my wife if I didn't handle it properly.

When you know a big move is right and that you'll drown otherwise, stick to your guns. You're no good to anyone else if you're at the bottom of the ocean.

While cutting weight sounds scary, it feels liberating in practice. Have you ever been overwhelmed and canceled a plan or appointment, then felt like you could breathe again? It's a great feeling! There's a little guilt from canceling, followed by the immense freedom of knowing you finally have some time for yourself. Guess what—when you canceled that plan, you escaped a tiny little overwhelm current and gave yourself a tiny bit of relief.

The more you cut weight, the more relief you get. As with every technique in the H.E.L.P. method, the relief you get from this will feel *so good* and *so right* that you'll find the courage to keep going! Guided by your feelings, you'll continue to set boundaries, granting yourself more and more relief. And as you come out the other side, you'll find that you can offer more to others than you ever did before.

I mean, look at me! I had to give up dinner parties, cut down on hanging out with friends, quit social media, and quit my job! Do you know how terrifying all of that was? It was super terrifying! I was so afraid that I was a failure, and that I was letting everyone down, particularly Preetha.

Now, a few years later, I'm a talented house manager who wrote and published a book! I work hard to advocate for my writing and earn money through book sales and coaching. I run a business for my wife so that her art gets turned into professional prints that end up on people's walls. I attend fancy social events and talk to people, knowing that I have the skills to recharge on my own terms because I've got help on the way.

Most importantly, I felt *relief* even before I had these successes under my belt, and now I experience *lasting relief* in the scenarios where before I felt overwhelmed!

You won't be able to seek H.E.L.P. without cutting weight. Keeping yourself buoyant keeps your head above water.

FLOATING, SWIMMING PARALLEL, AND CUTTING WEIGHT ONLY WORK IF YOU'RE SEEKING HELP!

I'd like to close this chapter with one final reminder that none of these activities will work if you aren't seeking the help described in the previous chapter. You may be tempted to do this chapter's activities with a perfectionist mindset. Do them instead with a survivalist mindset. You only goal is to survive until help gets there. Help is the answer—these activities are just what you do to stay afloat while you wait for help to come.

When done without help, these activities become panic activities that create a false sense of progress, which becomes evident when you inevitably spiral downward into an over-whelm current.

No matter how many skills you develop, no matter how good at self-soothing you are, and no matter how much weight you cut, without asking for help you will not succeed. In fact, you'll end up like I was before I learned to ask for help. I was even more lonely and resentful because I thought that taking personality tests, improving my skills, soothing myself, and limiting socializing entitled me to success. But when the success didn't come, I felt upset and confused, and just as overwhelmed as before.

At this point, fill out the portion of the H.E.L.P. worksheet shown below.

I will start using the following float behaviors:

_____

I will start using the following parallel swim behaviors: _____

I will lovingly cut weight by setting these boundaries:

_____

At this point, you've made it through H.E.L.P.! Now it's time to move to the final chapter, where we examine what a life lived in the H.E.L.P. method—a life on the beach—looks like.

CHAPTER EIGHT

LIFE IS GOOD ON THE BEACH

Y ou've been through the H.E.L.P. method, and now it's time to enjoy your reward of life at the beach.

Remember, getting H.E.L.P. is not a one-time thing. While you've used your first pass through the book to address one overwhelm current, you will constantly be pulled into more overwhelm currents that require attention. Each time you find yourself panicking or drowning in the face of overwhelm, simply pull out a new H.E.L.P. worksheet. It will ground you and set you on right path. Each time you escape another overwhelm current using H.E.L.P., life feels a little more like a relaxing day on the beach.

In this final section, we'll look at how getting help means we end up on the beach, but not always where we thought we would be. Life on the beach is good regardless of where we are. We'll see that we don't lose ourselves in this process despite the fact that our accomplishments depend on others. And we'll learn that getting help actually lets us unleash our true individuality.

LIFE IS GOOD ANYWHERE ON THE BEACH

Let's start by looking at how anywhere on the beach of life is a great place to be. I bring up this point because when a swimmer is rescued from a rip current, they don't end up at exactly the same place on the shore as they had been. The swimmer doesn't mind, however: they're so relieved to be alive, they don't care where they land! I believe that living life to escape overwhelm currents works the same way—wherever you end up, you can feel relieved and at peace.

I used to think that I had to get to an exact point in life to be happy. I thought achievements and status were what would bring ultimate happiness, so I had to go straight for them, directly against my overwhelm. I tried hard to look perfect physically, to present a successful façade for my coaching business, and to get my personal finances in exactly the right spot. Obviously that life didn't work out at all. Nowadays I'm happy just to live life day by day, accepting what comes and enjoying each moment.

Before I used the H.E.L.P. method, I went to bed every night thinking that maybe tomorrow would be the day I finally felt good enough. Now I go to bed thinking that I did my best, and that if I died in my sleep at night, I wouldn't have a single regret. That's a powerful feeling! And it didn't come from accomplishments. It came from getting so much wonderful help.

I don't have to worry about the past anymore because I know that I'm doing the therapy and support group work to resolve my trauma. I don't have to worry about the future because the more help I get, the more amazing life becomes. I may not know how things are going to turn out, but every day I feel that good things can't help but happen to me. Not because I'm special, but because there are so many wonderful human beings in my life helping me succeed. And I help them back.

Life on the beach is a great life.

IS BEACH LIFE BORING? AM I USELESS IF I NEED HELP WITH EVERYTHING?

I'd like to alleviate the worry that if all your overwhelm currents are handled with help from others, you'll be bored or feel a lack of purpose. I think boredom and lack of purpose come from being trapped in overwhelm currents and drowning, not from being at the beach. When you use H.E.L.P., you don't lose your individuality or your personal mark on the world. Instead, it's enhanced. You don't become bored—you become excited and invigorated.

I think this whole fear of losing our marks and getting bored is also tied to the disconnect between how we treat "physical" life and how we treat "mental" life. I've put those in quotes because I believe that life is life—it all operates under the same rules. Our mental life is still physical; it's our physical brain creating our thoughts, and the brain is a physical organ. In the physical world, we accept basic help without question. We accept utilities like water and electricity from our providers, we accept cars and public transport from manufacturers and governments, and we accept vaccines and healthcare from the medical field. We don't worry that accepting running water instead of going to the local well makes us less capable. We don't worry that driving a car instead of grooming and raising our own horses makes us dependent on others. That's because utilities, transportation, and medical services cover our bases so that we can express our individuality. We can do more with help, not less.

The same is true for mental health; society just doesn't realize it yet. When you accept help from an umbrella person, you can try more things. When you accept support from a peer group, you can live more freely and express your emotions better. When you accept therapy and consider medication with your doctor, you can live out your dreams while enjoying a peaceful, beach-like existence.

At the end of this book, there's an acknowledgements section. I thank dozens of individuals for helping me with my book, along with hundreds of launch team members. You might think that writing a book is a massive individual accomplishment. But the truth is, I needed enormous amounts of help to get this book out to you. The only thing I did was willingly ask for help, then express my individual experience and wisdom to you. That's what asking for help looks like— you become more engaged, more excited, more individualistically expressive—not less. I'm leaving my mark on the world thanks to the H.E.L.P. method, and you can too.

Getting Help Makes You a Giver, Not a Taker

I want to close this chapter by acknowledging that to get the help you need to become less overwhelmed, you will need to ask a lot from people. You are asking for a lot from an umbrella person, from a support group, and from your therapist. You will probably need to spend money, possibly money shared with another person, in order to get the help you need. You'll also need to take more time for yourself to do your floating and parallel swim behaviors, and you'll need to cut some weight along the way. You may be nervous that doing all this asking makes you a taker, someone who doesn't care about others.

I'd like to take a moment to address your hesitations. If your results are anything like mine, you'll end up using H.E.L.P. to create a much more robust social network. You'll be more involved in others' lives and more able to help them. You'll even end up helping the people who help you! You'll be a great mutual umbrella buddy with someone, a great member of a peer group, and a great client for your therapist.

You'll also become a person who exudes calm and safety instead of panic and drowning. Others will start to look to you as a leader and someone they want to be around. By helping yourself, you'll be helping many other people in your network. There are too few examples of people who exude calm and safety in the world, so you'll stand out as someone who's a little bit different. All these things mean you'll be an amazing help to those around you.

Consider me: I've asked for an enormous amount of help over the past few years, and as a result I've been able to publish this book, which will help many people. Despite the fact that I challenged Preetha by taking time away from social obligations and work, I've actually become much more of an asset to her at home, and my relationship with her is better than ever! And when I go onto social media and talk now, I feel like I'm being genuinely helpful to others and genuinely connecting instead of being overwhelmed and weighed down by social pressure. I'm so glad that I asked for help, and I think you will be too.

Getting H.E.L.P. doesn't make you a taker—it makes you one of the biggest givers out there!

Go Forth and H.E.L.P. Yourself and the World!

You've made it! You've learned about how society traps us in overwhelm currents, how to use the H.E.L.P method to escape them, and how to enjoy life on the beach. Give yourself a pat on the back. Then, in true H.E.L.P. fashion, go give a hug to everyone who helped you get to where you are now. Thank your parents, your teachers, your friends, and everyone who made your life possible. You are not a result of individual accomplishment. You are a product of help, and it's time for you to embrace it! When you do, you will help not only yourself but everyone around you. The world needs the best version of you, and the best version of you needs H.E.L.P. to get there!

At this point, all that's left to do is pull out your H.E.L.P. worksheet and commit to living it. If you've skipped any sections, go back and fill them in. If you're ready to get going, then you can write the final commitment below.

Go forth and H.E.L.P.!

–Woody

At this point, you can finish your H.E.L.P. worksheet by writing the affirmation below.

I, _____ am ready to live a life based on asking for help. I'm willing to use my H.E.L.P. method daily to reduce my overwhelm. I am excited to live my best life! Let's do this!

Signature:_____ Date: _____

APPENDIX: WORKSHEETS AND RESOURCES

H.E.L.P. WORKSHEET (BLANK)

I am overwhelmed by: _____

I panic in these ways:

- Fighting/creating conflict: _____

- People pleasing: _____

- Overwhelm-based criticism: _____

- Perfectionism: _____

- Other panic behaviors: _____

I, _____, accept that _____ (the overwhelm from line one) is an overwhelm current that is stronger than me. I am fully willing to give up these panic behaviors and accept help.

I use the following activities to drown my emotions:

Physical pleasure: _____

Screen time: _____

Busyness: _____

I, _____, accept that I have been drowning my emotions. I accept that the drowning behaviors listed above are harmful. I believe that my emotions are there to help me. I'm willing to engage them.

I, _____, accept that I need help. I am willing to ask for help.

The person I would like to ask to be my umbrella person is:

_____

I will ask them via _____(text, phone, in person), at this time: _____

The peer group I would like to join is: _____

The first meeting I will attend is on _____ (day) at _____

_____ (time), and is located at _____

(physical or online meeting location).

I am willing and open to receive professional help.

The type of professional help I need is: _____. I will ask my umbrella person _____ to help me engage them by doing this: _____

I will start using the following float behaviors:

_____

I will start using the following parallel swim behaviors:

_____

I will lovingly cut weight by setting these boundaries:

_____

I, _____, am ready to live a life based on asking for help. I'm willing to use my H.E.L.P. method daily to reduce my overwhelm. I am excited to live my best life! Let's do this!

Signature: _____   Date: _____

H.E.L.P. Worksheet (Filled Example)

I am overwhelmed by: <u>Being stuck in my career as a computer programmer</u>

I panic in these ways:

- Fighting/creating conflict: <u>Arguing with my boss about getting a promotion</u>
- People pleasing: <u>Being afraid to leave my desk because I might miss someone's message</u>
- Overwhelm-based criticism: <u>Telling myself I should be better at computer programming</u>
- Perfectionism: <u>Trying to make my emails, presentations, and meetings all perfect</u>
- Other panic behaviors: <u>Ranting about how upset I am about work to my wife</u>

I, <u>Woody</u>, accept that <u>being stuck in my career</u> is an overwhelm current that is stronger than me. I am fully willing to give up these panic behaviors and accept help.

I use the following activities to drown my emotions:

Physical pleasure: <u>Drinking alcohol alone, overeating takeout food</u>

Screen time: <u>Playing video games for hours on end, binge-watching television</u>

Busyness: <u>Obsessively helping others with work projects, trying to solve others' problems</u>

I, <u>Woody</u>, accept that I have been drowning my emotions. I accept that the drowning behaviors listed above are harmful. I believe that my emotions are there to help me. I'm willing to engage them.

I, Woody, accept that I need help. I am willing to ask for help.

The person I would like to ask to be my umbrella person is: <u>Preetha</u>

I will ask them via in person (text, phone, in person), at this time: 8 p.m. tonight

The peer group I would like to join is: Triangle Professionals in Career Transition

The first meeting I will attend is on this Saturday (day) at 4 p.m. (time), and is located at:

my favorite coffee house downtown (physical or online meeting location).

I am willing and open to receive professional help.

The type of professional help I need is: a therapist. I will ask my umbrella person Preetha to help me engage them by: Googling therapists near me

I will start using the following float behaviors: Headspace meditation, walks in nature

I will start using the following parallel swim behaviors: Taking personality tests, learning gardening

I will lovingly cut weight by setting these boundaries: No dinner parties until I get therapy for social anxiety

I, Woody, am ready to live a life based on asking for help. I'm willing to use my H.E.L.P. method daily to reduce my overwhelm. I am excited to live my best life! Let's do this!

Signature: *Woody Rini*   Date: 11/24/2016

BIBLIOGRAPHY

7 Cups (website), 7 Cups of Tea, accessed May 26, 2022.
https://www.7cups.com/.

911 At Ease International (website), accessed May 26, 2022.
https://911aei.org/.

B. Chris Brewster, Richard E. Gould, and Robert W.
Brander. "Estimations of rip current rescues and
drowning in the United States." *Natural Hazards and
Earth System Sciences* 19 (February 2019): 389–397.
https://doi.org/10.5194/nhess-19-389-2019.

"Binge." *Merriam-Webster.com Dictionary*, Merriam-
Webster, accessed May 26, 2022. https://www.merriam-
webster.com/dictionary/binge.

"Drug Abuse Statistics." National Center for Drug Abuse
Statistics, accessed May 26, 2022.
https://drugabusestatistics.org/.

"Career Transition." Meetup, accessed May 26,
2022.https://www.meetup.com/topics/career-transition/.

"Find an Affiliate." Mental Health America, accessed May
26, 2022. https://arc.mhanational.org/find-an-affiliate.

Gutentag, Tony, and Christa S. C. Asterhan. "Burned-out: Middle School Teachers after One Year of Online Remote Teaching during COVID-19." *Frontiers In Psychology*, March 10, 2022. https://www.frontiersin.org/articles/10.3389/fpsyg.2022.802520/full.

"List of suicide crisis lines." Wikipedia, last modified May 24, 2022, 15:47. https://en.wikipedia.org/wiki/List_of_suicide_crisis_lines.

"List of twelve-step groups." Wikipedia, last modified March 4, 2022, 20:42. https://en.wikipedia.org/wiki/List_of_twelve-step_groups.

"Medication." Mental Health America, accessed May 26, 2022. https://www.mhanational.org/medication.

"Mental Health." Center for Disease Control, accessed May 26, 2022. https://www.cdc.gov/nchs/fastats/mental-health.htm

"NAMI Peer-to-Peer." National Alliance on Mental Illness, accessed May 26, 2022. https://www.nami.org/Support-Education/Mental-Health-Education/NAMI-Peer-to-Peer.

"Panic." *Merriam-Webster.com Dictionary*, Merriam-Webster, accessed May 26, 2022. https://www.merriam-webster.com/dictionary/panic.

"SAMHSA's National Helpline." Substance Abuse and Mental Health Services Administration, last modified March 25, 2022. https://www.samhsa.gov/find-help/national-helpline.

Terlizzi, Emily P. and Benjamin Zablotsky. "Mental Health Treatment Among Adults: United States, 2019." *NCHS Data Brief* 380, (September 2020): https://www.cdc.gov/nchs/products/databriefs/db380.htm.

United States National Suicide Prevention Lifeline (website), Substance Abuse and Mental Health Services Administration, accessed May 26, 2022. https://suicidepreventionlifeline.org.

"Virtual Parent Support Groups." Parents Helping Parents, accessed May 26, 2022. https://www.parentshelpingparents.org/virtual-support-groups.

"Your Journey." National Alliance on Mental Illness, accessed May 26, 2022. https://nami.org/Your-Journey.

ACKNOWLEDGEMENTS

In true H.E.L.P. fashion, I needed a small army of people to publish this book. Getting *Help! I'm Overwhelmed!* out to the world required all the energy I had and more, and I am so grateful to everyone who helped me along the way.

Thank you to my mother, Ellen, for raising me to have energy and enthusiasm. And for being my number-one publicist!

Thank you to my father, Martin, for cultivating in me the creative spirit of inquiry that led to the discoveries documented in this book.

Thank you to my sisters, Sarah and Lucy, for working as extra moms as I was growing up.

Thank you to my wife, Preetha, for suffering through all of my crazy while I tried to convince the world I had something worth saying. And for being the best partner in life that anyone could ever have. I'd like to think that after working this hard on myself, I've become half of the person that you already are.

Thanks to Sara Loy for being an incredible editor, and for telling me not to throw my book in the trash.

Thanks to Jason Flores for telling me to get my book back out of the trash after I threw it in anyway.

Thanks to my advance copy readers: Ellen, Prathiba, Elizabeth, Sam, Adam, Ramasu, Tim, Priya, Jordan, Sarah, Lucy, Susan, Elaine, Beverly, Bridgette, Jane, Tyhgita, Olivia, Beth, Tammie, Carol, Mackenzie, Dana, Matt, Opal, Laura, Ann, Sarah, Kristol, Jenny, Xander, Emily, Yvonne, and Ruby.

Thanks to the wider launch team of 100+ people, who are too many to name individually and too awesome to measure individually. Every single one of you means the world to me.

Thanks to the new friends I made as I explored my own mental health challenges in 2021. Without your support, I would never have come close to publishing this book, but the truth is you've given me far more than a book—you've given me a new life. I owe you so much more than I can ever give back, but I'll try.

Thanks to every teacher, professor, guidance counselor (including Mom—wow, you're getting a lot of mentions!), and student advisor who helped me grow up to be an educated and caring person. I'm more you than I am me.

Thanks to every therapist, counselor, coach, doctor, psychiatrist, and specialist who has taken care of me so that I have been able to take care of others.

Finally, special thanks to dog Willie for being the loving presence I needed to complete my work, and for warning me whenever I get a package. And special thanks to dog Daphne for teaching me that it's okay to grieve a lost relationship, and that sometimes things don't work out even when we try our best.

And thanks to you, reader, for reading this book. I hope you learned something that will help yourself and others.

ABOUT THE AUTHOR

Woody Rini lives with his wife, Preetha, and their dog, Willie, in North Carolina. They enjoy seeing local sights and making friends with local parrots.

HELP OTHERS DISCOVER THE POWER OF H.E.L.P. BY LEAVING A REVIEW!

If *Help! I'm Overwhelmed!* was helpful to you, please leave a review on Amazon and help me spread the message that it's okay to ask for help! Your honest review may provide the information needed to help someone else change their life. Your feedback also helps me develop content that will help more people in the future.

Your honest Amazon review matters!

Thanks so much for going on this journey with me!

—Woody

Made in the USA
Middletown, DE
17 June 2022

67346840R00080